A NATURE POEM FOR
EVERY DAY OF THE YEAR

A NATURE POEM FOR EVERY DAY OF THE YEAR

EDITED BY *Jane McMorland Hunter*

BATSFORD

First published in the United Kingdom in 2018 by
B.T. Batsford
43 Great Ormond Street
London WC1N 3HZ

An imprint of B.T. Batsford Holdings Ltd

ISBN 978-1-84994-500-4

A CIP catalogue record for this book is available from the British Library.

10 9

Reproduction by Mission Productions Ltd, Hong Kong
Printed and bound by Toppan Leefung Printing Ltd, China

This book can be ordered direct from the publisher
at www.batsford.com, or try your local bookshop

Illustrations by Tatiana Boyko

CONTENTS

To Lily and Matilda, with love.

I found the poems in the fields
and only wrote them down.

John Clare

FURTHER READING

The following books bring our seasons to life, not just in poetry but through history, mythology, folklore and literature. This anthology would have been poorer without them:

Nick Groom, *The Seasons: A Celebration of the English Year*, Atlantic Books, 2013

Lia Leendertz, *The Almanac: A Seasonal Guide to 2018*, Unbound, 2017

John Lewis-Stempel, *Meadowland: The Private Life of an English Field*, Doubleday, 2014

The Wood: The Life and Times of Cockshutt Wood, Doubleday, 2018

ABOUT THE EDITOR

Jane McMorland Hunter has compiled five anthologies: *Favourite Poems of London*, *Favourite Poems of England* and *Classic Readings and Poems* for Batsford and *Poems of the First World War* and *Favourite Poems* for the National Trust. She also writes gardening books and works as a gardener and at Hatchards bookshop in Piccadilly as the Shop Scribe, compiling their annual catalogues.

Introduction

The sound of birdsong at dawn, rolling hills bathed in sunshine, piles of crisp golden leaves and snow falling silently: each signifies a particular time of year. Much of our countryside may no longer be truly 'wild', and our seasons may no longer conform to the reliable patterns we would like, but we all want to dream. As many of us are now slightly removed from nature, living in towns and cities and working away from the land, these dreams become ever more important.

As a nation the British have always been particularly bound to the seasons, rituals marking the significant moments of the year. It is only comparatively recently that we have, to a certain extent, subdued nature and the seasons, allowing us to regard the wilder aspects of our land through rose-tinted glasses. Poets from Geoffrey Chaucer and Michael Drayton to Ted Hughes and Alice Oswald have taken inspiration from our untamed landscapes, preserving glimpses of nature in verse.

Poetry is often read as an escape, and the perfect way to start, or end, each day are a few moments of escape into the natural world. This anthology contains a poem for every day, watching the natural world as it progresses through the seasons. Spring is a time of hope, a season of new life with William Wordsworth's daffodils, Andrew Young's mad March hares and Christina Rossetti's birdsong. Summer shifts into a time of leisure with long idyllic holidays in the countryside remembered from childhood. According to Henry James, the two most beautiful words in the English language were 'summer afternoon', a sentiment echoed by Emily Dickinson, Robert Browning and a host of other poets. Even nature seems to know that summer is a time to relax, with flowers nodding their heads, trees rustling gently in the breeze and the sun creating long shadows as evening draws to a close. John Keats, William Blake and W. H. Auden are the poets we associate with autumn, and this is possibly the most poetic season. The natural world, and the human one, hold onto the last lingering memories of summer before they turn to face the oncoming hardships of winter. George Crabbe and George Meredith perfectly frame this time of year with their yellow leaves and red berries. Winter can be savoured in poetry, rather than endured; bleak grey days are transformed into a world of glittering frost and snow-blanketed landscapes. Even in the darkest days life continues and soon we can turn our attention to the rebirth of spring.

If one wants to plough a field one would read an agricultural manual. The point of the poetry here is to give an imaginative view of nature: owls marry pussycats, carved leopards leap into life and snow is always deep and crisp. Even though I know that tigers do not roam our fields, you are unlikely to see a phoenix and crocodiles do not inhabit our rivers, I have included them. Opinion is divided regarding enchanted woods and the Loch Ness Monster, and these too have earned a place in this anthology. Geography is not strictly accurate either; Rachel Lyman Field's geese are more likely to be flying towards Britain rather than away from it. The point of these poems is that one can imagine. Many of the very best nature poems were actually written by educated town dwellers, relying on visits, memories or fantasy for their inspiration. It is no coincidence that so many nature poems were written during the

Industrial Revolution, a time when an idealised and often sentimental view of rural life and Britain's wild places became important.

Nature is often the starting point for a poem concerned with love, loss, life or death. Anne Batten Cristall's *Song* is obviously more than a description of seasons, just as Henry King's *A Contemplation upon Flowers* concerns more than a simple description of spring blooms. Whether it is the subject or the inspiration, nature is an important part of these poems.

In previous anthologies I have always, where possible, included the entire poem. For various reasons here many poems are reduced to an extract. Some were simply too long to include in their entirety. Others offer brief but vivid descriptions of the natural world within a poem. I have extracted these images, even if it means taking them out of their context. My hope is that readers will be inspired to seek out the entire poem.

Animals, birds, flowers, trees, the sea and the sky allow our imaginations to soar. This can only improve our lives:

What would the world be, once bereft
Of wet and of wildness? Let them be left,
O let them be left, wildness and wet;
Long live the weeds and the wilderness yet.
From *Inversnaid* by Gerard Manley Hopkins

JANUARY

Chill Airs and Wintry Winds

The Year's at the Spring

FROM *PIPPA PASSES*

The year's at the spring,
And day's at the morn;
Morning's at seven;
The hill-side's dew-pearled;
The lark's on the wing;
The snail's on the thorn;
God's in His heaven –
All's right with the world!

Robert Browning (1812–1889)

Eclogue I: The Months

FROM *BASIL AND EDWARD*

JANUARY

    Ed. The moon that mounts the sun's deserted way,
Turns the long winter night to a silver day;
But setteth golden in face of the solemn sight
Of her lord arising upon a world of white.

FEBRUARY

    Ba. I have in my heart a vision of spring begun
In a sheltering wood, that feels the kiss of the sun:
And a thrush adoreth the melting day that dies
In clouds of purple afloat upon saffron skies.

MARCH

    Ed. Now carol the birds at dawn, and some new lay
Announceth a homecome voyager every-day.
Beneath the tufted sallows the streamlet thrills
With the leaping trout and the gleam of the daffodils.

APRIL

    Ba. Then laugheth the year; with flowers the meads are bright;
The bursting branches are tipped with flames of light:
The landscape is light; the dark clouds flee above,
And the shades of the land are a blue that is deep as love.

MAY

    Ed. But if you have seen a village all red and old
In cherry-orchards a-sprinkle with white and gold,
By a hawthorn seated, or a witch-oelm flowering high,
A gay breeze making riot in the waving rye!

JUNE

    Ba. Then night retires from heaven; the high winds go
A-sailing in cloud-pavilions of cavern'd snow.
O June, sweet Philomel sang thy cradle-lay;
In rosy revel thy spirit shall pass away.

JULY

    Ed. Heavy is the green of the fields, heavy the trees
With foliage hang, drowsy the hum of bees
In the thund'rous air: the crowded scents lie low:
Thro' tangle of weeds the river runneth slow.

AUGUST

    Ba. A reaper with dusty shoon and hat of straw
On the yellow field, his scythe in his armës braw:
Beneath the tall grey trees resting at noon
From sweat and swink with scythe and dusty shoon.

SEPTEMBER

    Ed. Earth's flaunting flower of passion fadeth fair
To ripening fruit in sunlit veils of the air,
As the art of man makes wisdom to glorify
The beauty and love of life born else to die.

OCTOBER

    Ba. On frosty morns with the woods aflame, down, down
The golden spoils fall thick from the chestnut crown.
May Autumn in tranquil glory her riches spend,
With mellow apples her orchard-branches bend.

NOVEMBER

Ed. Sad mists have hid the sun, the land is forlorn:
The plough is afield, the hunter windeth his horn.
Dame Prudence looketh well to her winter stores,
And many a wise man finds his pleasure indoors.

DECEMBER

Ba. I pray thee don thy jerkin of olden time,
Bring us good ice, and silver the trees with rime;
And I will good cheer, good music and wine bestow,
When the Christmas guest comes galloping over the snow.

Robert Bridges (1844–1930)

To a Snowflake

What heart could have thought you? –
Past our devisal
(O filigree petal!)
Fashioned so purely,
Fragilely, surely,
From what Paradisal
Imagineless metal,
Too costly for cost?
Who hammered you, wrought you,
From argentine vapor? –
'God was my shaper.
Passing surmisal,
He hammered, He wrought me,
From curled silver vapor,
To lust of His mind –
Thou could'st not have thought me!
So purely, so palely,
Tinily, surely,
Mightily, frailly,
Insculped and embossed,
With His hammer of wind,
And His graver of frost.'

Francis Thompson (1859–1907)

Paradise Lost

BOOK VII, LINES 387–416

And God said, 'Let the waters generate
Reptile with spawn abundant, living soul;
And let fowl fly above the earth, with wings
Displayed on the open firmament of heaven.'
And God created the great whales, and each
Soul living, each that crept, which plenteously
The waters generated by their kinds,
And every bird of wing after his kind,
And saw that it was good, and blessed them, saying,
'Be fruitful, multiply, and in the seas
And lakes and running streams the waters fill;
And let the fowl be multiplied on the earth.'
Forthwith the sounds and seas, each creek and bay,
With fry innumerable swarm, and shoals
Of fish with their fins and shining scales
Glide under the green wave, in sculls that oft
Bank the mid-sea; part, single or with mate,
Graze the sea-weed, their pasture, and through groves
Of coral stray, or sporting with quick glance
Show to the sun their waved coats dropped with gold,
Or in their pearly shells at ease, attend
Moist nutriment, or under rocks their food
In jointed armour watch; on smooth the seal
And bended dolphins play: part, huge of bulk,
Wallowing unwieldy, enormous in their gait,
Tempest the ocean: there leviathan
Hugest of living creatures, on the deep
Stretched like a promontory slaps or swims,
And seems a moving land, and at his gills
Draws in, and at his trunk spouts out, a sea.

John Milton (1608–1674)

The Seasons

FROM *THE FAERIE QUEEN*, MUTABILITY
CLAIMS TO RULE THE WORLD, LINES 136–171

So, forth issew'd the Seasons of the yeare;
    First, lusty Spring, all dight in leaues of flowres
    That freshly budded and new bloosmes did beare
    (In which a thousand birds had built their bowres
    That sweetly sung, to call forth Paramours):
    And in his hand a iauelin did beare,
    And on his head (as fit for warlike stoures)
    A guilt engrauen morion he did weare;
That as some did him loue, so others did him feare.

Then came the iolly Sommer, being dight
    In a think silken cassock coloured greene,
    That was vnlyned all, to be more light:
    And on his head a girlond well beseene
    He wore, from which as he had chauffed been
    The sweat did drop; and in his hand he bore
    A boawe and shaftes, as he in forrest greene
    Had hunted late the Libbard or the Bore,
And now would bathe his limbs, with labor heated sore.

Then came the Autumne all in yellow clad,
    As though he ioyed in his plenteous store,
    Laden with fruits that made him laugh, full glad
    That he had banisht hunger, which to-fore
    Had by the belly oft him pinched sore.
    Vpon his head a wreath that was enrold
    With eares of corn, of euery sort he bore:
    And in his hand a sickle he did holde,
To reape the ripened fruits the which the earth had yold.

Lastly, came Winter cloathed all in frize,
    Chattering his teeth for cold that did him chill,
    Whil'st on his hoary beard his breath did freese;
    And the dull drops that from his purpled bill
    As from a limbeck did adown distill.
    In his right hand a tipped staffe he held,
    With which his feeble steps he stayed still:
    For, he was faint with cold, and weak with eld;
That scares his loosed limbes he hable was to weld.

Edmund Spenser (c. 1552–1599)

God's Grandeur

The world is charged with the grandeur of God.
    It will flame out, like shining from shook foil;
    It gathers to a greatness, like the ooze of oil
Crushed. Why do men then now not reck his rod?
Generations have trod, have trod, have trod;
    And all is seared with trade; bleared, smeared with toil;
    And wears man's smudge and shares man's smell: the soil
Is bare now, nor can foot feel, being shod.

And for all this, nature is never spent;
    There lives the dearest freshness deep down things;
And though the last lights off the black West went
    Oh, morning, at the brown brink eastward, springs –
Because the Holy Ghost over the bent
    World broods with warm breast and with ah! bright wings.

Gerard Manley Hopkins (1844–1889)

Woods in Winter

When winter winds are piercing chill,
    And through the hawthorn blows the gale,
With solemn feet I tread the hill,
    That overbrows the lonely vale.

O'er the bare upland, and away
    Through the long reach of desert woods,
The embracing sunbeams chastely play
    And gladden these deep solitudes.

Where, twisted round the barren oak,
    The summer vine in beauty clung,
And summer winds the stillness broke,
    The crystal icicle is hung.

Where, from their frozen urns, mute springs
    Pour out the river's gradual tide,
Shrilly the skater's iron rings,
    And voices fill the woodland side.

Alas! how changed from the fair scene,
    When birds sang out their mellow lay,
And winds were soft, and woods were green,
    And the song ceased not with the day!

But still wild music is abroad,
    Pale, desert woods! within your crowd;
And gathering winds, in hoarse accord,
    Amid the vocal reeds pipe loud.

Chill airs and wintry winds! my ear
   Has grown familiar with your song;
I hear it in the opening year,
   I listen, and it cheers me long.

Henry Wadsworth Longfellow (1807–1882)

January is the first month in the year

1

January is the first month in the year
When the weather is cold and clear:
Boys roll the snowball round and round
Or slide on the pond where the ice is sound.

2

February Fill-ditch then sets in
With a pelting rain that will wet you to the skin
Soon as the sky shews a speck of blue
How the pretty snowdrops gleam to view.

3

March comes on with wind from the East,
A wind good neither for man nor beast:
The daffodil flaunts it in yellow and green
What cares she if the wind be keen?

4

April's showers and sunshine bright
Paint the rainbow to our sight:
Then the violet smelling sweet
Under every hedge we meet.

5

May hangs blossoms on the thorn –
Then the lamb and colt are born:
Primroses forsaken die
Gaudier flowers engage the eye.

6

June with tulips, eglantine
Will be finest of the fine:
Rose and lily odours yield
New-made hay scents many a field.

7

In July the sultry night
Scarce will cool the weary wight:
Then the woolly sheep are shorn
Then the harvest home is borne.

8

August brings the juicy grape
Melons too of goodly shape:
Then the melting peaches come
Nectarine apple pear and plum.

9

In September hares must die
Grouse and partridge swift and shy:
Then's the time to hunt and shoot
Then's the time to gather fruit.

10

In October drink good ale
Soon the year begins to fail:
Drink the ale so fine and mellow
Though the leaves are turning yellow.

11

Chill November's surly blast
Tears the boughs and drives them fast:
Then the sleet mixed up with rain
Makes us of the wet complain.

12

Cold December's frosty air
Makes us to the fire repair:
Then good friends each other meet
To enjoy a Christmas treat.

Sara Coleridge (1802–1852)

The Fallow Deer at the Lonely House

One without looks in to-night
    Through the curtain-chink
From the sheet of glistening white;
One without looks in to-night
    As we sit and think
    By the fender-brink.

We do not discern those eyes
    Watching in the snow;
Lit by lamps of rosy dyes
We do not discern those eyes
    Wondering, aglow
    Four-footed, tiptoe.

Thomas Hardy (1840–1928)

The Sky is low – the Clouds are mean

The Sky is low – the Clouds are mean.
A Travelling Flake of Snow
Across a Barn or through a Rut
Debates if it will go –

A Narrow Wind complains all Day
How some one treated him
Nature, like Us, is sometimes caught
Without her Diadem.

Emily Dickinson (1830–1886)

On the Phoenix

Come, Phoenix, come, if such a bird there be,
Point me out the happy tree,
Whose boughs can boast they bear the nest
Wherein thou lov'st to rest:
O lead me to the envied place,
Which thou dost with thy presence grace.

Arabia boasts she is the spot of earth
Wherein thou first got birth.
Dost thou never change thy clime
In so vast a space of time?
What entertainment hast thou there,
That is not any other where?
Come westward, noble bird, and see
What homage we will pay to thee.

But hark! I hear Arabia's sons reply:
'We enjoy tranquillity
In a more enlarged extent
Than any other continent;
We possess a richer soil,
With less labour and less toil,
    Than any men below,
And live at greater distance from a foe.

'Our stately trees all kinds of spices bear,
Our fountains gratify the ear,
Each leaf in consort joins to please
With the soft whispers of the evening breeze.
Here doth Phoebus make his bed,
'Tis by him she's hither led:

Why should not we the honour have
To her a residence to give?

'To our blest land did Nature send the fire
In which her mother did expire:
Five hundred years she's lived a chaste exile,
Then died upon the funeral pile;
Out of her fragrant ashes came
This exalted bird of fame;
To Phoebus' burning rays she owes her life;
In his chaste arms her mother died, ere she was made a wife.'

Such fables oft are told of thee,
Yet I confess thou seems to me
A bird begot by Poetry.
Thousands have beheld thee on
The fabled mountain Helicon:
    'Tis there thou loves to dwell.
Nay, I myself have seen thee there,
But never any other where,
    Except at Pindar's well.

Jean Adams (1710–1765)

England

We have no grass locked up in ice so fast
That cattle cut their faces and at last,
When it is reached, must lie them down and starve,
With bleeding mouths that freeze too hard to move.
We have not that delirious state of cold
That makes men warm and sing when in Death's hold.
We have no roaring floods whose angry shocks
Can kill the fishes dashed against the rocks.
We have no winds that cut down street by street,
As easy as our scythes can cut down wheat.
No mountains here to spew their burning hearts
Into the valleys, on our human parts.
No earthquakes here, that ring church bells afar,
A hundred miles from where those earthquakes are.
We have no cause to set our dreaming eyes,
Like Arabs, on fresh streams in Paradise.
We have no wilds to harbour men that tell
More murders than they can remember well.
No woman here shall wake from her night's rest,
To find a snake is sucking at her breast.
Though I have travelled many and many a mile,
And had a man to clean my boots and smile
With teeth that had less bone in them than gold –
Give me this England now for all my world.

W. H. Davies (1871–1940)

The Snow-Storm

Announced by all the trumpets of the sky,
Arrives the snow, and, driving o'er the fields,
Seems nowhere to alight: the whited air
Hides hills and woods, the river, and the heaven,
And veils the farm-house at the garden's end.
The sled and traveller stopped, the courier's feet
Delayed, all friends shut out, the housemates sit
Around the radiant fireplace, enclosed
In a tumultuous privacy of storm.

Come see the north wind's masonry.
Out of an unseen quarry evermore
Furnished with tile, the fierce artificer
Curves his white bastions with projected roof
Round every windward stake, or tree, or door.
Speeding, the myriad-handed, his wild work
So fanciful, so savage, nought cares he
For number or proportion. Mockingly,
On coop or kennel he hangs Parian wreaths;
A swan-like form invests the hidden thorn;
Fills up the farmer's lane from wall to wall,
Maugre the farmer's sighs; and, at the gate,
A tapering turret overtops the work.
And when his hours are numbered, and the world
Is all his own, retiring, as he were not,
Leaves, when the sun appears, astonished Art
To mimic in slow structures, stone by stone,
Built in an age, the mad wind's night-work,
The frolic architecture of the snow.

Ralph Waldo Emerson (1803–1882)

To a Snowdrop

Lone Flower, hemmed in with snows and white as they
But hardier far, once more I see thee bend
Thy forehead, as if fearful to offend,
Like an unbidden guest. Though day by day,
Storms, sallying from the mountain-tops, waylay
The rising sun, and on the plains descend;
Yet art thou welcome, welcome as a friend
Whose zeal outruns his promise! Blue-eyed May
Shall soon behold this border thickly set
With bright jonquils, their odours lavishing
On the soft west-wind and his frolic peers;
Nor will I then thy modest grace forget,
Chaste Snowdrop, venturous harbinger of Spring,
And pensive monitor of the fleeting years!

William Wordsworth (1770–1850)

January

FROM *THE SHEPHERD'S CALENDAR*

Again the robin waxes tame
And ventures pitys crumbs to claim
Picking the trifles off the snow
Which dames on purpose daily throw
And perching on the window sill
Where memory recollecting still
Knows the last winters broken pane
And there he hops and peeps again
The clouds of starnels dailey fly
Blackening thro the evening sky
To whittleseas reed wooded mere
And ozier holts by rivers near
And many a mingld swarthy crowd
Rook crow and jackdaw noising loud
Fly too and fro to dreary fen
Dull winters weary flight agen
Flopping on heavy wings away
As soon as morning wakens grey
And when the sun sets round and red
Returns to naked woods to bed
Wood pigeons too in flocks appear
By hunger tamd from timid fear
They mid the sheep unstartld steal
And share wi them a scanty meal
Picking the green leaves want bestows
Of turnips sprouting thro the snows.

John Clare (1793–1864)

The Keener Tempest

FROM *WINTER, THE SEASONS*

The keener tempests come: and fuming dun
From all the livid east, or piercing north,
Thick clouds ascend; in whose capacious womb
A vapoury deluge lies, to snow congeal'd.
Heavy they roll their fleecy world along;
And the sky saddens with the gather'd storm.
Through the hush'd air the whitening shower descends,
At first thin wavering; till at last the flakes
Fall broad, and wide, and fast, dimming the day
With a continual flow. The cherish'd fields
Put on their winter robe of purest white.

James Thomson (1700–1748)

Weathers

I

This is the weather the cuckoo likes,
    And so do I;
When showers betumble the chestnut spikes,
    And nestlings fly:
And the little brown nightingale bills his best,
And they sit outside at 'The Travellers' Rest',
And maids come forth sprig-muslin drest,
And citizens dream of the south and west,
    And so do I.

II

This is the weather the shepherd shuns,
    And so do I;
When beeches drip in browns and duns,
    And thresh, and ply;
And hill-hid tides throb, throe on throe,
And meadow rivulets overflow,
And drops on gate-bars hang in a row,
And rooks in families homeward go,
    And so do I.

Thomas Hardy (1840–1928)

The Rainbow

Even the rainbow has a body
made of drizzling rain
and it is an architecture of glistening atoms
built up, built up
yet you can't lay your hand on it,
nay, nor even your mind.

D. H. Lawrence (1885–1930)

Blow, Blow, Thou Winter Wind

FROM *AS YOU LIKE IT*, ACT II, SCENE VII

Blow, blow, thou winter wind,
Thou art not so unkind
 As man's ingratitude;
Thy tooth is not so keen,
Because thou art not seen,
 Although thy breath be rude.
Hey-ho, sing hey-ho, unto the green holly.
Most friendship is feigning, most loving mere folly:
 Then, hey-ho, the holly;
 This life is most jolly.

Freeze, freeze, thou bitter sky,
That dost not bite so nigh
 As benefits forgot:
Though thou the waters warp,
Thy sting is not so sharp
 As friend remembered not.
Hey-ho, sing hey-ho, unto the green holly.
Most friendship is feigning, most loving mere folly:
 Then, hey-ho, the holly;
 This life is most jolly.

William Shakespeare (1564–1616)

Seasons

Oh the cheerful budding-time
    When thorn-hedges turn to green;
When new leaves of elm and lime
    Cleave and shed their winter screen:
Tender lambs are born and baa,
    North wind finds no snow to bring,
Vigorous nature laughs Haha
    In the miracle of spring.

Oh the gorgeous blossom-days
    When broad flag-flowers drink and blow;
In and out in summer blaze
    Dragonflies flash to and fro:
Ashen branches hang out keys,
    Oaks put forth the rosy shoot,
Wandering herds wax sleek at ease,
    Lovely blossoms end in fruit.

Oh the shouting harvest-weeks:
    Mother Earth grown fat with sheaves;
Thrifty gleaner finds who seeks:
    Russet golden pomp of leaves
Crowns the woods, to fall at length;
    Bracing winds are felt to stir,
Ocean gathers up her strength,
    Beasts renew their dwindled fur.

Oh the starving winter-lapse
    Ice-bound, hunger-pinched and dim:
Dormant roots recal their saps,
    Empty nests show black and grim,
Short-lived sunshine gives no heat,
    Undue buds are nipped by frost,
Snow sets forth a windingsheet,
    And all hope of life seems lost.

Christina Rossetti (1830–1894)

Forsaken Woods

Forsaken woods, trees with sharpe storms opprest
whose leaves once hidd, the sun, now strew the grownd
once bred delight, now scorn, late usde to sownd
of sweetest birds, now of hoars crowes the nest

Gardens which once in thowsand coulers drest
shewed natures pryde: now in dead sticks abownd
in whome prowde summers treasure late was found
now but the rags, of winters torn coate rest

Medows whose sydes, late fayre brookes kist now slyme
embraced holds: feelds whose youth green and brave
promist long lyfe, now frosts lay in the grave

Say all and I with them: what doth not tyme!
but they whoe knew tyme, tyme will finde again
I that fayre tymes lost, on tyme call in vain.

Robert Sidney, Earl of Leicester (1563–1626)

Out in the Dark

Out in the dark over the snow
The fallow fawns invisible go
With the fallow doe;
And the winds blow
Fast as the stars are slow.

Stealthily the dark haunts round
And, when the lamp goes, without sound
At a swifter bound
Than the swiftest hound,
Arrives, and all else is drowned;

And star and I and wind and deer,
Are in the dark together, – near,
Yet far, – and fear
Drums on my ear
In that sage company drear.

How weak and little is the light,
All the universe of sight,
Love and delight,
Before the might,
If you love it not, of night.

Edward Thomas (1878–1917)

Snow Storm

Winter is come in earnest and the snow
In dazzling splendour – crumping underfoot
Spreads a white world all calm and where we go
By hedge or wood trees shine from top to root
In feathered foliage flashing light and shade
Of strangest contrast – fancys pliant eye
Delighted sees a vast romance displayed
And fairy halls descended from the sky
The smallest twig its snowy burthen wears
And woods oer head the dullest eyes engage
To shape strange things – where arch and pillar bears
A roof of grains fantastic arched and high
And little shed beside the spinney wears
The grotesque zemblance of an hermitage

One almost sees the hermit from the wood
Come bending with his sticks beneath his arm
And then the smoke curl up its dusky flood
From the little white roof his peace to warm
One shapes his books his quiet and his joys
And in romances world forgetting mood
The scene so strange so fancys mind employs
It seems heart aching for his solitude
Domestic spots near home and trod so oft
Seen daily – known for years – by the strange wand
Of winters humour changed – the little croft
Left green at night when morns loth look obtrudes
Tree bushes grass to one wild garb subdued
Are gone and left us in another land.

John Clare (1793–1864)

On Wenlock Edge

A SHROPSHIRE LAD, XXXI

On Wenlock Edge the wood's in trouble;
　His forest fleece the Wrekin heaves;
The gale, it plies the saplings double,
　And thick on Severn snow the leaves.

'Twould blow like this through holt and hanger
　When Uricon the city stood:
'Tis the old wind in the old anger,
　But then it threshed another wood.

Then, 'twas before my time, the Roman
　At yonder heaving hill would stare:
The blood that warms an English yeoman,
　The thoughts that hurt him, they were there.

There, like the wind through woods in riot,
　Through him the gale of life blew high;
The tree of man was never quiet:
　Then 'twas the Roman, now 'tis I.

The gale, it plies the saplings double,
　It blows so hard, 'twill soon be gone:
To-day the Roman and his trouble
　Are ashes under Uricon.

A. E. Housman (1859–1936)

Farewell to the Highlands

My heart's in the Highlands, my heart is not here;
My heart's in the Highlands a chasing the deer;
A chasing the wild deer, and following the roe,
My heart's in the Highlands wherever I go.
Farewell to the Highlands, farewell to the north,
The birth place of Valour, the country of Worth,
Wherever I wander, wherever I rove,
The hills of the Highlands for ever I love.

Farewell to the mountains high cover'd with snow;
Farewell to the straths and green vallies below:
Farewell to the forests and wild hanging woods;
Farewell to the torrents and loud pouring floods.
My heart's in the Highlands, my heart is not here,
My heart's in the Highlands a chasing the deer:
Chasing the wild deer, and following the roe,
My heart's in the Highlands wherever I go.

Robert Burns (1759–1796)

The Snow-drop

VERSE 1

Fear no more, thou timid Flower!
Fear thou no more the winter's might,
The whelming thaw, the ponderous shower,
The silence of the freezing night!
Since Laura murmur'd o'er thy leaves
The potent sorceries of song,
To thee, meek Flowret! gentler gales
    And cloudless skies belong.

Samuel Taylor Coleridge (1772–1834)

Triad I

I

The word of the sun to the sky,
 The word of the wind to the sea,
  The word of the moon to the night,
   What may it be?

II

The sense to the flower of the fly,
 The sense of the bird to the tree,
  The sense to the cloud of the light,
   Who can tell me?

III

The song of the fields to the kye,
 The song of the lime to the bee,
  The song of the depths to the height,
   Who knows all three?

Algernon Charles Swinburne (1837–1909)

Ode to the Snow-drop

The Snow-drop, Winter's timid child,
　　Awakes to life, bedew'd with tears,
And flings around its fragrance mild;
And where no rival flow'rets bloom,
Amid the bare and chilling gloom,
　　A beauteous gem appears!

All weak and wan, with head inclin'd,
　　Its parent-breast the drifted snow,
It trembles, while the ruthless wind
Bends its slim form; the tempest lowers,
Its em'rald eye drops crystal show'rs
　　On its cold bed below.

Poor flow'r! on thee the sunny beam
　　No touch of genial warmth bestows!
Except to thaw the icy stream
　　Whose little current purls along,
　　Thy fair and glossy charms among,
And whelms thee as it flows.

The night-breeze tears thy silky dress,
　　Which deck'd, with silv'ry lustre shone;
The morn returns, not thee to bless,
　　The gaudy *Crocus* flaunts its pride,
　　And triumphs where *its rival* – died,
　　Unshelter'd and unknown!

No sunny beam shall gild thy grave,
    No bird of pity thee deplore;
There shall noverdant branches wave;
        For spring shall all her gems unfold,
        And revel 'midst her beds of gold,
    When thou art seen no more!

Where'er I find thee, gentle flow'r,
    Thou still art sweet, and dear to me!
For I have known the cheerless hour,
        Have seen the sun-beams cold and pale,
        Have felt the chilling, wint'ry gale,
    And wept, and shrunk like thee!

Mary Robinson (1758–1800)

Winter Heavens

Sharp is the night, but stars with frost alive
Leap off the rim of earth across the dome.
It is a night to make the heavens our home
More than the nest whereto apace we strive.
Lengths down our road each fir-tree seems a hive,
Its swarms outrushing from the golden comb.
They waken waves of thoughts that burst to foam:
The living throb in me, the dead revive.
Yon mantle clothes us: there, past mortal breath,
Life glistens on the river of the death.
It folds us, flesh and dust; and have we knelt.
Or never knelt, or eyed as kine the springs
Of radiance, the radiance enrings:
And this is the soul's haven to have felt.

George Meredith (1828–1909)

Birds at Winter Nightfall

(TRIOLET)

Around the house the flakes fly faster,
And all the berries now are gone
From holly and cotoneaster
Around the house. The flakes fly! – faster
Shutting indoors that crumb-outcaster
We used to see upon the lawn
Around the house. The flakes fly faster,
And all the berries now are gone!

Thomas Hardy (1840–1928)

A Year's Windfalls

On the wind of January
    Down flits the snow,
Travelling from the frozen North
    As cold as it can blow.
Poor robin redbreast,
    Look where he comes;
Let him in to feel your fire,
    And toss him of your crumbs.

On the wind in February
    Snowflakes float still,
Half inclined to turn to rain,
    Nipping, dripping, chill.
Then the thaws swell the streams,
    And swollen rivers swell the sea: –
If the winter ever ends
    How pleasant it will be.

In the wind of windy March
    The catkins drop down,
Curly, caterpillar-like,
    Curious green and brown.
With concourse of nest-building birds
    And leaf-buds by the way,
We begin to think of flowers
    And life and nuts some day.

With the gusts of April
    Rich fruit-tree blossoms fall,
On the hedged-in orchard-green,
    From the southern wall.

Apple trees and pear trees
    Shed petals white or pink,
Plum trees and peach trees;
    While sharp showers sink and sink.

Little brings the May breeze
    Beside pure scent of flowers,
While all things wax and nothing wanes
    In lengthening daylight hours.
Across the hyacinth beds
    The wind lags warm and sweet,
Across the hawthorn tops,
    Across the blades of wheat.

In the wind of sunny June
    Thrives the red-rose crop,
Every day fresh blossoms blow
    While the first leaves drop;
White rose and yellow rose
    And moss rose choice to find,
And the cottage cabbage rose
    Not one whit behind.

On the blast of scorched July
    Drives the pelting hail,
From thunderous lightning-clouds, that blot
    Blue heaven grown lurid-pale.
Weedy waves are tossed ashore,
    Sea-things strange to sight
Gasp upon the barren shore
    And fade away in light.

In the parching August wind
    Cornfields bow the head,
Sheltered in round valley depths,
    On low hills outspread.
Early leaves drop loitering down
    Weightless on the breeze,
First fruits of the year's decay
    From the withering trees.

In brisk wind of September
    The heavy-headed fruits
Shake upon their bending boughs
    And drop from the shoots;
Some glow golden in the sun,
    Some show green and streaked,
Some set forth a purple bloom,
    Some blush rosy-cheeked.

In strong blast of October
    At the equinox,
Stirred up in his hollow bed
    Broad ocean rocks;
Plunge the ships on his bosom,
    Leaps and plunges the foam, –
It's oh! for mothers' sons at sea,
    That they were safe at home.

In slack wind of November
  The fog forms and shifts;
All the world comes out again
  When the fog lifts.
Loosened from their sapless twigs
  Leaves drop with every gust;
Drifting, rustling, out of sight
  In the damp or dust.

Last of all, December,
  The year's sands nearly run,
Speeds on the shortest day,
  Curtails the sun;
With its bleak raw wind
  Lays the last leaves low,
Brings back the nightly frosts,
  Brings back the snow.

Christina Rossetti (1830–1894)

FEBRUARY

The Last Hours of Slow Winter

Ceremonies for Candlemasse Eve

Down with the Rosemary and Bayes,
    Down with the Mistleto;
In stead of Holly, now up-raise
    The greener Box (for show).

Holly hitherto did sway;
    Let Box now domineere;
Untill the dancing Easter-day,
    Or Easters Eve appeare.

Then youthfull Box which now hath grace,
    Your houses to renew;
Grown old, surrender must his place,
    Unto the crisped Yew.

When Yew is out, then Birch comes in,
    And many Flowers beside;
Both of a fresh, and fragrant kinne
    To honour Whitsontide.

Green Rushes then, and sweetest Bents,
    With cooler Oken boughs;
Come in for comely ornaments,
    To re-adorn the house.
Thus times do shift; each thing his turne do's hold;
New things succeed, as former things grow old.

Robert Herrick (1591–1674)

The Fork of the Road

An utter moorland, high, and wide, and flat;
A beaten roadway, branching out in grave distaste;
And weather-beaten and defaced,
Pricking its ears along the solitary waste –
A signpost; pointing this way, pointing that.

William Renton (fl. 1875–1905)

Snow

PARTS I AND II

I

'Who affirms that crystals are alive?'
    I affirm it, let who will deny: –
Crystals are engendered, wax and thrive,
    Wane and wither: I have seen them die.

Trust me, masters, crystals have their day
    Eager to attain the perfect norm,
Lit with purpose, potent to display
    Facet, angle, colour, beauty, form.

II

Water-crystals need for flower and root
    Sixty clear degrees, no less, no more;
Snow, so fickle, still in this acute
    Angle thinks, and learns no other lore:

Such its life, and such its pleasure is,
    Such its art and traffic, such its gain,
Evermore in new conjunctions this
    Admirable angle to maintain.

Crystalcraft in every flower and flake
    Snow exhibits, of the welkin free:
Crystalline are crystals for the sake,
    All and singular, of crystalry.

Yet does every crystal of the snow
    Individualise, a seedling sown
Broadcast, but instinct with power to grow
    Beautiful in beauty of its own.

Every flake with all its prongs and dints
    Burns ecstatic as a new-lit star:
Men are not more diverse, finger prints
    More dissimilar than snow-flakes are.

Worlds of men and snow endure, increase,
    Woven of power and passion to defy
Time and travail: only races cease,
    Individual men and crystals die.

John Davidson (1857–1909)

Snow-Flakes

Out of the bosom of the Air,
    Out of the cloud-folds of her garments shaken,
Over the woodlands brown and bare,
    Over the harvest-fields forsaken,
       Silent, and soft, and slow
       Descends the snow.

Even as our cloudy fancies take
    Suddenly shape in some divine expression,
Even as the troubled heart doth make
    In the white countenance confession,
       The troubled sky reveals
       The grief it feels.

This is the poem of the air,
    Slowly in silent syllables recorded;
This is the secret of despair,
    Long in its cloudy bosom hoarded,
       Now whispered and revealed
       To wood and field.

Henry Wadsworth Longfellow (1807–1882)

Winter Seascape

The sea runs back against itself
    With scarcely time for breaking wave
To cannonade a slatey shelf
    And thunder under in a cave

Before the next can fully burst.
    The headwind, blowing harder still,
Smooths it to what it was at first –
    A slowly rolling water-hill.

Against the breeze the breakers haste,
    Against the tide their ridges run
And all the sea's a dappled waste
    Criss-crossing underneath the sun.

Far down the beach the ripples drag
    Blown backward, rearing from the shore,
And wailing gull and shrieking shag
    Alone can pierce the ocean roar.

Unheard, a mongrel hound gives tongue,
    Unheard are shouts of little boys:
What chance has any inland lung
    Against this multi-water noise?

Here where the cliffs alone prevail
    I stand exultant, neutral, free,
And from the cushion of the gale
    Behold a huge consoling sea.

John Betjeman (1906–1984)

Seal Lullaby

FROM *THE JUNGLE BOOK*

Oh! hush thee, my baby, the night is behind us,
    And black are the waters that sparkled so green.
The moon, o'er the combers, looks downward to find us
    At rest in the hollows that rustle between.
Where billow meets billow, there soft be thy pillow;
    Ah, weary wee flipperling, curl at thy ease!
The storm shall not wake thee, nor shark overtake thee,
    Asleep in the arms of the slow-swinging seas.

Rudyard Kipling (1865–1936)

Let the Fog Rise

the fog enveloped us shortly after four.
by the edge of the copse I stumbled:
reaching for the dark earth my fingers fled
into the obdurate loam.

a nesting of pale sibilant eggs, quite hidden.
hands digging deeper now, searching:
searching for some unknown cache;
hunting some unseen curvature.

Joel Knight (1975–)

What art thou, Frost?

FROM *WINTER, THE SEASONS*

What art thou, frost? and whence are thy keen stores
Derived, thou secret all-invading power,
Whom e'en the illusive fluid cannot fly?
Is not thy potent energy, unseen,
Myriads of little salts, or hook'd, or shaped
Like double wedges, and diffused immense
Through water, earth, and ether? Hence at eve,
Steam'd eager from the red horizon round,
With the fierce rage of Winter deep suffused,
An icy gale, oft shifting, o'er the pool
Breathes a blue film, and in its mid career
Arrests the bickering stream. The loosen'd ice,
Let down the flood and half-dissolved by day,
Rustles no more; but to the sedgy bank
Fast grows, or gathers round the pointed stone,
A crystal pavement, by the breath of Heaven
Cemented firm; till, seized from shore to shore,
The whole imprison'd river growls below.

James Thomson (1700–1748)

At Middle-Field Gate in February

The bars are thick with drops that show
    As they gather themselves from the fog
Like silver buttons ranged in a row,
And as evenly spaced as if measured, although
    They fall at the feeblest jog.

They load the leafless hedge hard by,
    And the blades of last year's grass,
While the fallow ploughland turned up nigh
In raw rolls clammy and clogging lie –
    Too clogging for feet to pass.

How dry it was on a far-back day
    When straws hung the hedge and around,
When amid the sheaves in amorous play
In curtained bonnets and light array
    Bloomed a bevy now underground!

Thomas Hardy (1840–1928)

Celandine

Thinking of her had saddened me at first,
Until I saw the sun on the celandines lie
Redoubled, and she stood up like a flame,
A living thing, not what before I nursed,
The shadow I was growing to love almost,
The phantom, not the creature with bright eye
That I had thought never to see, once lost.

She found the celandines of February
Always before us all. Her nature and name
Were like those flowers, and now immediately
For a short swift eternity back she came,
Beautiful, happy, simply as when she wore
Her brightest bloom among the winter hues
Of all the world; and I was happy too,
Seeing the blossoms and the maiden who
Had seen them with me Februarys before,
Bending to them as in and out she trod
And laughed, with locks sweeping the mossy sod.

But this was a dream; the flowers were not true,
Until I stooped to pluck from the grass there
One of five petals and I smelt the juice
Which made me sigh, remembering she was no more,
Gone like a never perfectly recalled air.

Edward Thomas (1878–1917)

Written with a Pencil

STANDING BY THE FALL OF FYERS, NEAR LOCH-NESS

Among the heathy hills and ragged woods
The roaring Fyers pours his mossy floods;
Till full he dashes on the rocky mounds,
Where, thro' a shapeless breach, his stream resounds.
As high in air the bursting torrents flow,
As deep recoiling surges foam below,
Prone down the rock the whitening sheet descends,
And viewless Echo's ear, astonish'd, rends.
Dim-seen, thro' rising mists and ceaseless show'rs,
The hoary cavern, wide-surrounding lours.
Still thro' the gap the struggling river toils,
And still, below, the horrid caldron boils.

Robert Burns (1759–1796)

The Sound of the Sea

The sea awoke at midnight from its sleep,
    And round the pebbly beaches far and wide
    I heard the first wave of the rising tide
    Rush onward with uninterrupted sweep;
A voice out of the silence of the deep,
    A sound mysteriously multiplied
    As of a cataract from the mountain's side,
    Or roar of winds upon a wooded steep.
So comes to us at times, from the unknown
    And inaccessible solitudes of being,
    The rushing of the sea-tides of the soul;
And inspirations, that we deem our own,
    Are some divine foreshadowing and foreseeing
    Of things beyond our reason or control.

Henry Wadsworth Longfellow (1807–1882)

The Owl and the Pussycat

The Owl and the Pussycat went to sea
    In a beautiful pea-green boat,
They took some honey, and plenty of money,
    Wrapped up in a five-pound note.
The Owl looked up to the stars above,
    And sang to a small guitar,
'O lovely Pussy! O Pussy, my love,
    What a beautiful Pussy you are,
        You are,
        You are!
What a beautiful Pussy you are!'

Pussy said to the Owl, 'You elegant fowl!
    How charmingly sweet you sing!
O let us be married! too long we have tarried:
    But what shall we do for a ring?'
They sailed away, for a year and a day,
    To the land where the Bong-tree grows,
And there in a wood a Piggy-wig stood,
With a ring at the end of his nose,
        His nose,
        His nose.
With a ring at the end of his nose.

'Dear Pig, are you willing to sell for one shilling
    Your ring?' Said the Piggy, 'I will.'
So they took it away and were married next day
    By the Turkey who lives on the hill.
They dined on mince, and slices of quince,
    Which they ate with a runcible spoon;
And hand in hand, on the edge of the sand
    They danced by the light of the moon,
        The moon,
        The moon,
They danced by the light of the moon.

Edward Lear (1812–1888)

Seynt Valentynes Day

FROM *THE PARLIAMENT OF FOWLS*, LINES 302–315

And in a launde, upon an hille of floures,
Was set this noble goddesse Nature;
Of braunches were hir halles and hir boures,
Y-wrought after hir craft and hir mesure;
Ne ther nas foul that cometh of engendrure,
That they ne were prest in hir presence,
To take hir doom and yeve hir audience.

For this was on seynt Valentynes day,
Whan every foul cometh ther to chese his make,
Of every kinde, that men thenke may;
And that so huge a noyse gan they make,
That erthe and see, and tree, and every lake
So ful was, that unnethe was ther space
For me to stonde, so ful was al the place.

Geoffrey Chaucer (c. 1343–1400)

To the Small Celandine

VERSES 1–5

Pansies, lilies, kingcups, daisies,
Let them live upon their praises;
Long as there's a sun that sets,
Primroses will have their glory;
Long as there are violets,
They will have a place in story:
There's a flower that shall be mine,
'Tis the little Celandine.

Eyes of some men travel far
For the finding of a star;
Up and down the heavens they go,
Men that keep a mighty rout!
I'm as great as they, I trow,
Since the day I found thee out,
Little Flower! – I'll make a stir,
Like a sage astronomer.

Modest, yet withal an Elf
Bold, and lavish of thyself;
Since we needs must first have met
I have seen thee, high and low,
Thirty years or more, and yet
'Twas a face I did not know;
Thou hast now, go where I may,
Fifty greetings in a day.

Ere a leaf is on a bush,
In the time before the thrush
Has a thought about her nest,
Thou wilt come with half a call,
Spreading out thy glossy breast
Like a careless Prodigal;
Telling tales about the sun,
When we've little warmth, or none.

Poets, vain men in their mood!
Travel with the multitude:
Never heed them; I aver
That they all are wanton wooers;
But the thrifty cottager,
Who stirs little out of doors,
Joys to spy thee near her home;
Spring is coming! Thou are come!

William Wordsworth (1770–1850)

February – A Thaw

VERSE 1

The snow is gone from cottage tops
The thatch moss glows in brighter green
And eves in quick succession drops
Where grinning icles once hath been
Pit patting wi a pleasant noise
In tubs set by the cottage door
While ducks and geese with happy joys
Douse in the yard pond brimming oer.

John Clare (1793–1864)

The Unloosening

Winter was weary. All his snows were failing –
Still from his stiff grey head he shook the rime
Upon the grasses, bushes and broad hedges,
But all was lost in the new touch of Time.

And the bright-globèd hedges were all ruddy,
As though warm sunset glowed perpetual.
The myriad swinging tassels of first hazel,
From purple to pale gold, were swinging all

In the soft wind, no more afraid of Winter.
Nor chaffinch, wren, nor lark was now afraid.
And Winter heard, or (ears too hard of hearing)
Snuffed the South-West that in his cold hair played.

And his hands trembled. Then with voice a-quaver
He called the East Wind, and the black East ran,
Roofing the sky with iron, and in the darkness
Winter crept out and chilled the earth again.

And while men slept the still pools were frozen,
Mosses were white, with ice the long grasses bowed;
The hawthorn buds and the greening honeysuckle
Froze, and the birds were dumb under that cloud.

And men and beasts were dulled, and children even
Less merry, under that low iron dome.
Early the patient rooks and starlings gathered;
Any warm narrow place for men was home.

And Winter laughed, but the third night grew weary,
And slept all heavy, till the East Wind thought him dead.
Then the returning South West in his nostrils
Breathed, and his snows melted. And his head

Uplifting, he saw all the laughing valley,
Heard the unloosened waters leaping down
Broadening over the meadows; saw the sun running
From hill to hill and glittering upon the town.

All day he stared. But his head drooped at evening,
Bent and slow he stumbled into the white
Cavern of a great chalk hill, hedged with tall bushes,
And in its darkness found a darker night

Among the broken cliff and falling water,
Freezing or falling quietly everywhere;
Locked in a long, long sleep, his brain undreaming,
With only water moving anywhere.

Old men at night dreamed that they saw him going,
And looked, and dared not look, lest he should turn.
And young men felt the air beating on their bodies,
And the young women woke from dreams that burn.

And children going through the fields at morning
Saw the unloosened waters leaping down,
And broke the hazel boughs and wore the tassels
Above their eyes – a pale and shaking crown.

John Freeman (1880-1929)

First Sight

Lambs that learn to walk in snow
When their bleating clouds the air
Meet a vast unwelcome, know
Nothing but a sunless glare.
Newly stumbling to and fro
All they find, outside the fold,
Is a wretched width of cold.

As they wait beside the ewe,
Her fleeces wetly caked, there lies
Hidden round them, waiting too,
Earth's immeasureable surprise.
They could not grasp it if they knew,
What so soon will wake and grow
Utterly unlike the snow.

Philip Larkin (1922–1985)

Winter Rain

Every valley drinks,
    Every dell and hollow:
Where the kind rain sinks and sinks,
    Green of Spring will follow.

Yet a lapse of weeks
    Buds will burst their edges,
Strip their wool-coats, glue-coats, streaks,
    In the woods and hedges;

Weave a bower of love
    For birds to meet each other,
Weave a canopy above
    Nest and egg and mother.

But for fattening rain
    We should have no flowers,
Never a bud or leaf again
    But for soaking showers;

Never a mated bird
    In the rocking tree-tops,
Never indeed a flock or herd
    To graze upon the lea-crops.

Lambs so woolly white,
    Sheep the sun-bright leas on,
They could have no grass to bite
    But for rain in season.

We should find no moss
    In the shadiest places,
Find no waving meadow grass
    Pied with broad-eyed daisies:

But miles of barren sand,
    With never a son or daughter,
Not a lily on the land,
    Or lily on the water.

Christina Rossetti (1830–1894)

The Cat and the Moon

The cat went here and there
And the moon spun round like a top,
And the nearest kin of the moon,
The creeping cat, looked up.
Black Minnaloushe stared at the moon,
For, wander and wail as he would,
The pure cold light in the sky
Troubled his animal blood.
Minnaloushe runs in the grass
Lifting his delicate feet.
Do you dance, Minnaloushe, do you dance?
When two close kindred meet,
What better than call a dance?
Maybe the moon may learn,
Tired of that courtly fashion,
A new dance turn.
Minnaloushe creeps through the grass
From moonlit place to place,
The sacred moon overhead
Has taken a new phase.
Does Minnaloushe know that his pupils
Will pass from change to change,
And that from round to crescent,
From crescent to round they range?
Minnaloushe creeps through the grass
Alone, important and wise,
And lifts to the changing moon
His changing eyes.

W. B. Yeats (1865–1939)

The Question

I

I dreamed that, as I wandered by the way,
    Bare Winter suddenly was changed to Spring,
And gentle odours led my steps astray,
    Mixed with a sound of waters murmuring
Along a shelving bank of turf, which lay
    Under a copse, and hardly dared to fling
Its green arms round the bosom of the stream,
But kissed it and then fled, as thou mightest in dream.

II

There grew pied wind-flowers and violets,
    Daisies, those pearled Arcturi of the earth,
The constellated flower that never sets;
    Faint oxlips; tender bluebells, at whose birth
The sod scarce heaved; and that tall flower that wets –
    Like a child, half in tenderness and mirth –
Its mother's face with Heaven's collected tears,
When the low wind, its playmate's voice, it hears.

III

And in the warm hedge grew lush eglantine,
    Green cowbind and the moonlight-coloured may,
And cherry-blossoms, and white cups, whose wine
    Was the bright dew, yet drained not by the day;
And wild roses, and ivy serpentine,
    With its dark buds and leaves, wandering astray;
And flowers azure, black, and streaked with gold,
Fairer than any wakened eyes behold.

IV

And nearer to the river's trembling edge
    There grew broad flag-flowers, purple pranked with white,
And starry river buds among the sedge,
    And floating water-lilies, broad and bright,
Which lit the oak that overhung the hedge
    With moonlight beams of their own watery light;
And bulrushes, and reeds of such deep green
As soothed the dazzled eye with sober sheen.

V

Methought that of these visionary flowers
    I made a nosegay, bound in such a way
That the same hues, which in their natural bowers
    Were mingled or opposed, the like array
Kept these imprisoned children of the Hours
    Within my hand, – and then, elate and gay,
I hastened to the spot whence I had come,
That I might there present it! – Oh! to whom?

Percy Bysshe Shelley (1792–1822)

Thaw

Over the land freckled with snow half-thawed
The speculating rooks at their nests cawed
And saw from elm-tops, delicate as flower of grass,
What we below could not see, Winter pass.

Edward Thomas (1878–1917)

First Sight of Spring

The hazel blooms in threads of crimson hue
Peep through the swelling buds and look for spring,
Ere yet a white thorn leaf appears in view
Or march finds throstles pleased enough to sing
On the old touchwood tree wood peckers cling
A moment and their harsh toned notes renew
In happier mood, the stockdove claps his wing
The squirrel sputters up the powdered oak
With tail cocked oer his head and ears erect
Startled to hear the woodmans understroke
And with the courage that his fears collect
He hisses fierce half malice and half glee
Leaping from branch to branch about the tree
In winters foliage moss and lichen drest

John Clare (1793–1864)

The Year's Awakening

How do you know that the pilgrim track
Along the belting zodiac
Swept by the sun in his seeming rounds
Is traced by now to the Fishes' bounds
And into the Ram, when weeks of cloud
Have wrapt the sky in a clammy shroud,
And never as yet a tinct of spring
Has shown in the Earth's apparelling;
　　O vespering bird, how do you know,
　　How do you know?

How do you know, deep underground,
Hid in your bed from sight and sound,
Without a turn in temperature,
With weather life can scarce endure,
That light has won a fraction's strength,
And day put on some moments' length,
Whereof in merest rote will come,
Weeks hence, mild airs that do not numb;
　　O crocus root, how do you know,
　　How do you know?

Thomas Hardy (1840–1928)

The Thaw-Wind

SONNET XCIX

Thro' the deep drifts the south wind breathed its way
Down to the earth's green face; the air grew warm,
The snow-drops had regain'd their lonely charm;
The world had melted round them in a day:
My heart full long'd for violets – the blue arch
Of heaven – the blackbird's song – but Nature kept
Her stately order – Vegetation slept –
Nor could I force the unborn sweet of March
Upon a winter's thaw. With eyes that brook'd
A narrower prospect than my fancy crav'd,
Upon the golden aconites I look'd,
And on the leafless willows as they wav'd –
And on the broad leav'd, half-thaw'd ivy-tod,
That glitter'd, dripping down upon the sod.

Charles Tennyson Turner (1808–1879)

Spring Quiet

Gone were but the Winter,
  Come were but the Spring,
I would go to a covert
  Where the birds sing;

Where in the whitethorn
  Singeth a thrush,
And a robin sings
  In the holly-bush.

Full of fresh scents
  Are the budding boughs
Arching high over
  A cool green house:

Full of sweet scents,
  And whispering air
Which sayeth softly:
  'We spread no snare;

'Here dwell in safety,
  Here dwell alone,
With a clear stream
  And a mossy stone.

'Here the sun shineth
    Most shadily;
Here is heard an echo
    Of the far sea,
    Tho' far off it be.'

Christina Rossetti (1830–1894)

Last Hours

A gray day and quiet,
   With slow clouds of gray,
And in dull air a cloud that falls, falls
      All day.

The naked and stiff branches
   Of oak, elm, thorn,
In the cold light are like men aged and
      Forlorn.

Only a gray sky,
   Grass, trees, grass again,
And all the air a cloud that drips, drips,
      All day.

Lovely the lonely
   Bare trees and green grass –
Lovelier now the last hours of slow winter
      Slowly pass.

John Freeman (1880–1929)

The Miracle

Come, sweetheart, listen, for I have a thing
Most wonderful to tell you – news of spring.

Albeit winter still is in the air,
And the earth troubled, and the branches bare,

Yet down the fields to-day I saw her pass –
The spring – her feet went shining through the grass.

She touched the ragged hedgerows – I have seen
Her finger-prints, most delicately green;

And she has whispered to the crocus leaves,
And to the garrulous sparrows in the eaves.

Swiftly she passed and shyly, and her fair
Young face was hidden in her cloudy hair.

She would not stay, her season is not yet,
But she has reawakened, and has set

The sap of all the world astir, and rent
Once more the shadows of our discontent.

Triumphant news – a miracle I sing –
The everlasting miracle of spring.

John Drinkwater (1882–1937)

The Year

The crocus, while the days are dark,
    Unfolds its saffron sheen;
At April's touch the crudest bark
    Discovers gems of green.

Then sleep the seasons, full of might;
    While slowly swells the pod
And rounds the peach, and in the night
    The mushroom bursts the sod.

The Winter falls; the frozen rut
    Is bound with silver bars;
The snow-drift heaps against the hut,
    And night is pierc'd with stars.

Coventry Patmore (1823–1896)

MARCH

I Heard a Thousand Blended Notes

The First Spring Day

I wonder if the sap is stirring yet,
If wintry birds are dreaming of a mate,
If frozen snowdrops feel as yet the sun
And crocus fires are kindling one by one:
　　Sing, robin, sing;
I still am sore in doubt concerning Spring.

I wonder if the springtide of this year
Will bring another Spring both lost and dear;
If heart and spirit will find out their Spring,
Or if the world alone will bud and sing:
　　Sing, hope, to me;
Sweet notes, my hope, soft notes for memory.

The sap will surely quicken soon or late,
The tardiest bird will twitter to a mate;
So Spring must dawn again with warmth and bloom,
Or in this world, or in the world to come:
　　Sing, voice of Spring,
Till I too blossom and rejoice and sing.

Christina Rossetti (1830–1894)

The Wren

Why is the cuckoos melody preferred
And nightingales rich song so fondly praised
In poets rhymes   Is there no other bird
Of natures minstrelsy that oft hath raised
Ones heart to extacy and mirth as well
I judge not how anothers taste is caught
With mine theres other birds that bear the bell
Whose song hath crowds of happy memories brought
Such the wood Robin singing in the dell
And little Wren that many a time hath sought
Shelter from showers in huts where I did dwell
In ealy spring the tenant of the plain
Tenting my sheep and still they come to tell
The happy stories of the past again.

John Clare (1793–1864)

The Three Winds

The hard blue winds of March
shake the young sheep
and flake the long stone walls;
now from the gusty grass
comes the horned music of rams,
and plovers fall out of the sky
filling their wings with snow.

Tired of this northern tune
the winds turn soft
blowing white butterflies
out of dog-rose hedges,
and schoolroom songs are full
of boy's green cuckoos
piping the summer round.

Till August sends at last
its brick-red breath
over the baking wheat and blistered poppy,
brushing with feathered hands
the skies of brass,
with dreams of river moss
my thirst's delirium.

Laurie Lee (1914–1997)

Song

Now the Spring is waking,
    Very shy as yet,
Busy mending, making
    Grass and violet,
Frowsy Winter's over;
    See the budding lane!
Go and meet your lover;
    Spring is here again!

Every day is longer
    Than the day before;
Lambs are whiter, stronger,
    Birds sing more and more;
Woods are less than shady,
    Griefs are more than vain –
Go and kiss your lady;
    Spring is here again!

E. Nesbit (1858–1924)

Within the Circuit of this Plodding Life

Within the circuit of this plodding life
There enter moments of an azure hue,
Untarnished fair as is the violet
Or anemone, when the spring stews them
By some meandering rivulet, which make
The best philosophy untrue that aims
But to console man for his grievences.
I have remembered when the winter came,
High in my chamber in the frosty nights,
When in the still light of the cheerful moon,
On the every twig and rail and jutting spout,
The icy spears were adding to their length
Against the arrows of the coming sun,
How in the shimmering noon of summer past
Some unrecorded beam slanted across
The upland pastures where the Johnswort grew;
Or heard, amid the verdure of my mind,
The bee's long smothered hum, on the blue flag
Loitering amidst the mead; or busy rill,
Which now through all its course stands still and dumb
Its own memorial, – purling at its play

Along the slopes, and through the meadows next,
Until its youthful sound was hushed at last
In the staid current of the lowland stream;
Or seen the furrows shine but late upturned,
And where the fieldfare followed in the rear,
When all the fields around lay bound and hoar
Beneath a thick integument of snow.
So by God's cheap economy made rich
To go upon my winter's task again.

Henry David Thoreau (1817–1862)

Lines Written in Early Spring

I heard a thousand blended notes,
While in a grove I sate reclined,
In that sweet mood when pleasant thoughts
Bring sad thoughts to the mind.

To her fair works did Nature link
The human soul that through me ran;
And much it grieved my heart to think
What man has made of man.

Through primrose tufts, in that green bower,
The periwinkle trailed its wreaths;
And 'tis my faith that every flower
Enjoys the air it breathes.

The birds around me hopped and played,
Their thoughts I cannot measure: –
But the least motion which they made
It seemed a thrill of pleasure.

The budding twigs spread out their fan,
To catch the breezy air;
And I must think, do all I can,
That there was pleasure there.

If this belief from heaven be sent,
If such be Nature's holy plan,
Have I not reason to lament
What man has made of man?

William Wordsworth (1770–1850)

A Backward Spring

The trees are afraid to put forth buds,
And there is timidity in the grass;
The plots lie gray where gouged by spuds,
    And whether next week will pass
Free of sly sour winds is the fret of each bush
    Of barberry waiting to bloom.

Yet the snowdrop's face betrays no gloom,
And the primrose pants in its heedless push,
Though the myrtle asks if it's worth the fight
    This year with frost and rime
    To venture one more time
On delicate leaves and buttons of white
From the selfsame bough as at last year's prime,
And never to ruminate on or remember
What happened to it in mid-December.

Thomas Hardy (1840–1928)

8 MARCH

Spring Snow

(A CINQUAIN)

Snowflakes
Slip from the sky
Like soft white butterflies,
Brush the trees with their flimsy wings,
Vanish.

John Foster (1941–)

Surly Winter Passes Off

FROM *SPRING, THE SEASONS*

And see where surly Winter passes off,
Far to the north, and calls his ruffian blasts:
His blasts obey, and quit the howling hill,
The shatter'd forest, and the ravaged vale;
While softer gales succeed, at whose kind touch,
Dissolving snows in livid torrents lost,
The mountains lift their green heads to the sky.

James Thomson (1700–1748)

Dipper

No webbed feet,
but a water bird for all that.

And a gentlemanly one –
he walks on the bottom
of his helter-skelter stream
wearing a white shirt front
and a brown cummerbund.

He hates dry land.
Flying up a twisty stream
he follows the twists
all the way.

When he perches on a stone
it's a wet one.
He stands there, bobbing and bobbing
as though the water's applauding him.

He likes his nest
to be a rippling tapestry –
a tapestry? Well,
a waterfall.

Naturally.

Norman MacCaig (1910–1996)

The Cataract of Lodore

'How does the water
Come down at Lodore?'
My little boy asked me
Thus, once on a time;
And moreover he tasked me
To tell him in rhyme.
Anon, at the word,
There first came one daughter,
And then came another,
To second and third
The request of their brother,
And to hear how the water
Comes down at Lodore,
With its rush and its roar,
As many a time
They had seen it before.
So I told them in rhyme,
For of rhymes I had store;
And 'twas in my vocation
For their recreation
That so I should sing;
Because I was Laureate
To them and the King.

From its sources which well
In the tarn on the fell;
From its fountains
In the mountains,
Its rills and its gills;
Through moss and through brake,
It runs and it creeps

For a while, till it sleeps
In its own little lake.
And thence at departing,
Awakening and starting,
It runs through the reeds,
And away it proceeds,
Through meadow and glade,
In sun and in shade,
And through the wood-shelter,
Among crags in its flurry,
Helter-skelter,
Hurry-skurry.
Here it comes sparkling,
And there it lies darkling;
Now smoking and frothing
Its tumult and wrath in,
Till, in this rapid race
On which it is bent,
It reaches the place
Of its steep descent.

The cataract strong
Then plunges along,
Striking and raging

As if a war raging
Its caverns and rocks among;
Rising and leaping,
Sinking and creeping,
Swelling and sweeping,
Showering and springing,

Flying and flinging,
Writhing and ringing,
Eddying and whisking,
Spouting and frisking,
Turning and twisting,
Around and around
With endless rebound:
Smiting and fighting,
A sight to delight in;
Confounding, astounding,
Dizzying and deafening the ear with its sound.

Collecting, projecting,
Receding and speeding,
And shocking and rocking,
And darting and parting,
And threading and spreading,
And whizzing and hissing,
And dripping and skipping,
And hitting and splitting,
And shining and twining,
And rattling and battling,
And shaking and quaking,
And pouring and roaring,
And waving and raving,
And tossing and crossing,
And flowing and going,
And running and stunning,
And foaming and roaming,
And dinning and spinning,
And dropping and hopping,

And working and jerking,
And guggling and struggling,
And heaving and cleaving,
And moaning and groaning;

And glittering and frittering,
And gathering and feathering,
And whitening and brightening,
And quivering and shivering,
And hurrying and skurrying,
And thundering and floundering;

Dividing and gliding and sliding,
And falling and brawling and sprawling,
And driving and riving and striving,
And sprinkling and twinkling and wrinkling,
And sounding and bounding and rounding,
And bubbling and troubling and doubling,
And grumbling and rumbling and tumbling,
And clattering and battering and shattering;

Retreating and beating and meeting and sheeting,
Delaying and straying and playing and spraying,
Advancing and prancing and glancing and dancing,
Recoiling, turmoiling and toiling and boiling,
And gleaming and streaming and steaming and beaming,
And rushing and flushing and brushing and gushing,
And flapping and rapping and clapping and slapping,
And curling and whirling and purling and twirling,
And thumping and plumping and bumping and jumping,
And dashing and flashing and splashing and clashing;

And so never ending, but always descending,
Sounds and motions for ever and ever are blending
All at once and all o'er, with a mighty uproar, –
And this way the water comes down at Lodore.

Robert Southey (1774–1843)

Endure Hardness

A cold wind stirs the blackthorn
    To burgeon and to blow,
Besprinkling half-green hedges
    With flakes and sprays of snow.

Thro' coldness and thro' keenness,
    Dear hearts, take comfort so:
Somewhere or other doubtless
    These make the blackthorn blow.

Christina Rossetti (1830–1894)

The Violet

Down in a green and shady bed,
A modest violet grew,
Its stalk was bent, it hung its head,
As if to hide from view.

And yet it was a lovely flower,
Its colours bright and fair;
It might have graced a rosy bower,
Instead of hiding there,

Yet there it was content to bloom,
In modest tints arrayed;
And there diffused its sweet perfume,
Within the silent shade.

Then let me to the valley go,
This pretty flower to see;
That I may also learn to grow
In sweet humility.

Jane Taylor (1783–1824)

The Lamb

Little Lamb who made thee?
   Dost thou know who made thee?
Gave thee life, and bid thee feed,
By the stream and o'er the mead;
Gave thee clothing of delight,
Softest clothing, woolly bright;
Gave thee such a tender voice,
Making all the vales rejoice?
   Little Lamb who made thee?
   Dost thou know who made thee?

Little Lamb, I'll tell thee,
   Little Lamb, I'll tell thee:
He is callèd by thy name,
For He calls Himself a Lamb.
He is meek and He is mild;
He became a little child.
I a child, and thou a lamb,
We are callèd by His name.
   Little Lamb, God bless thee!
   Little Lamb, God bless thee!

William Blake (1757–1827)

Magdalen Walks

The little white clouds are racing over the sky,
  And the fields are strewn with the gold of the flower of March,
  The daffodil breaks under foot, and the tasselled larch
Sways and swings as the thrush goes hurrying by.

A delicate odour is borne on the wings of the morning breeze,
  The odour of deep wet grass, and of brown new-furrowed earth,
  The birds are singing for joy of the Spring's glad birth,
Hopping from branch to branch on the rocking trees.

All the woods are alive with the murmur and sound of Spring,
  And the rosebud breaks into pink on the climbing briar,
  And the crocus-bed is a quivering moon of fire
Girdled round with the belt of an amethyst ring.

And the plane to the pine-tree is whispering some tale of love
  Till it rustles with laughter and tosses its mantle of green,
  And the gloom of the wych-elm's hollow is lit with the iris sheen
Of the burnished rainbow throat and the silver breast of a dove.

See! the lark starts up from his bed in the meadow there,
  Breaking the gossamer threads and the nets of dew,
  And flashing a-down the river, a flame of blue!
The kingfisher flies like an arrow, and wounds the air.

Oscar Wilde (1854–1900)

The Traveller

When March was master of furrow and fold,
And the skies kept cloudy festival,
And the daffodil pods were tipped with gold
And a passion was in the plover's call,
A spare old man went hobbling by
With a broken pipe and a tapping stick,
And he mumbles – 'Blossom before I die,
Be quick, you little brown buds, be quick.

'I've weathered the world for a count of years –
Good old years of shining fire –
And death and the devil bring no fears,
And I've fed the flame of my last desire;
I'm ready to go, but I'd pass the gate
On the edge of the world with an old heart sick
If I missed the blossoms. I may not wait –
The gate is open – be quick, be quick.'

John Drinkwater (1882–1937)

The Rainbow

    See on one hand
He drops his bright roots in the water'd sward,
And rosing part, on part dispenses green;
But with his other foot three miles beyond
He rises from the flocks of villages
That bead the plain; did ever Havering church-tower
Breathe in such ether? or the Quickly elms
Mask'd with such violet disallow their green.

Gerard Manley Hopkins (1844–1889)

Written in March

WHILE RESTING ON THE BRIDGE
AT THE FOOT OF BROTHER'S WATER

The Cock is crowing,
The stream is flowing,
The small birds twitter,
The lake doth glitter,
The green field sleeps in the sun;
The oldest and youngest
Are at work with the strongest;
The cattle are grazing,
Their heads never raising;
There are forty feeding like one!

Like an army defeated
The snow hath retreated,
And now doth fare ill
On the top of the bare hill;
The plowboy is whooping – anon – anon:
There's joy in the mountains;
There's life in the fountains;
Small clouds are sailing,
Blue sky prevailing;
The rain is over and gone!

William Wordsworth (1770–1850)

A Mill

Two leaps the water from its race
    Made to the brook below,
The first leap it was curving glass,
    The second bounding snow.

William Allingham (1824–1889)

Spring Equinox

Do not say, referring to the sun
'Its journey northward has begun,'
As though it were a bird, annually migrating,
That now returns to build in rich trees
Its nest of golden grass. Do not belie
Its lusty health with words such as imply
A pallid invalid recuperating.
The age demands the facts, therefore be brief –
Others will sense the simile – and say:
'We are turning towards the sun's indifferent ray.'

R. S. Thomas (1913–2000)

The Tyger

FROM *SONGS OF EXPERIENCE*

Tyger Tyger, burning bright,
In the forests of the night:
What immortal hand or eye,
Could frame thy fearful symmetry?

In what distant deeps or skies
Burnt the fire of thine eyes!
On what wings dare he aspire?
What the hand dare seize the fire?

And what shoulder, and what art,
Could twist the sinews of thy heart?
And when thy heart began to beat,
What dread hand? and what dread feet?

What the hammer? what the chain,
In what furnace was thy brain?
What the anvil? what dread grasp,
Dare its deadly terrors clasp?

When the stars threw down their spears
And water'd heaven with their tears:
Did he smile his work to see?
Did he who made the Lamb make thee?

Tyger Tyger, burning bright,
In the forests of the night:
What immortal hand or eye,
Dare frame thy fearful symmetry?

William Blake (1757–1827)

A Contemplation upon Flowers

Brave flowers, that I could gallant it like you
And be as little vaine;
You come abroad, and make a harmless shew,
And to your bedds of Earth againe;
You are not proud, you know your birth
For your Embroiderd garments are from Earth.

You doe obey your months, and times, but I
Would have it ever springe,
My fate would know noe winter, never dye,
Nor thinke of such a thing;
Oh that I could my bed of Earth but view
And Smile, and looke as chearefully as you:

Oh teach me to see death and not to feare
But rather to take truce;
How often have I seene you at a Beere,
And there looke fresh and spruce;
You fragrant flowers then teach me that my breath
Like yours may sweeten, and perfume my death.

Henry King (1592–1669)

The Primrose

FROM *QUEEN MAB*, CANTO IX, LINES 165–170

Though storms may break the primrose on its stalk,
Though frosts may blight the freshness of its bloom,
Yet Spring's awakening breath will woo the earth,
To feed with kindliest dews its favourite flower,
That blooms in mossy banks and darksome glens,
Lighting the greenwood with its sunny smile.

Percy Bysshe Shelley (1792–1822)

March Hares

I made myself as a tree,
No withered leaf twirling on me;
No, not a bird that stirred the boughs,
As looking out from wizard brows
I watched those lithe and lovely forms
That raised the leaves in storms.

I watched them leap and run,
Their bodies hollowed in the sun
To thin transparency,
That I could clearly see
The shallow colour of their blood
Joyous in love's full flood.

I was content enough,
Watching that serious game of love,
That happy hunting in the wood
Where the pursuer was the more pursued,
To stand in breathless hush
With no more life myself than tree or bush.

Andrew Young (1885–1971)

To Daffadills

Faire Daffadills, we weep to see
    You haste away so soone;
As yet the early-rising Sun
    Has not attain'd his Noone.
      Stay, stay,
    Untill the hasting day
          Has run
    But to the Even-song;
And, having pray'd together, we
    Will goe with you along.

We have short time to stay, as you,
    We have as short a Spring;
As quick a growth to meet Decay,
    As you, or any thing.
      We die
    As your hours doe, and drie
          Away,
    Like to the Summer's raine;
Or as the pearles of Morning's dew
    Ne'er to be found againe.

Robert Herrick (1591–1674)

The Raven

VERSES 1–8

Once upon a midnight dreary, while I pondered, weak and weary,
Over many a quaint and curious volume of forgotten lore –
While I nodded, nearly napping, suddenly there came a tapping,
As of someone gently rapping, rapping at my chamber door.
''Tis some visitor,' I muttered, 'tapping at my chamber door –
        Only this and nothing more.'

Ah, distinctly I remember it was in the bleak December;
And each separate dying ember wrought its ghost upon the floor.
Eagerly I wished the morrow; – vainly I had sought to borrow
From my books surcease of sorrow – sorrow for the lost Lenore –
For the rare and radiant maiden whom the angels name Lenore –
        Nameless *here* for evermore.

And the silken, sad, uncertain rustling of each purple curtain
Thrilled me – filled me with fantastic terrors never felt before;
So that now, to still the beating of my heart, I stood repeating
''Tis some visitor entreating entrance at my chamber door –
Some late visitor entreating entrance at my chamber door; –
        This it is and nothing more.'

Presently my soul grew stronger; hesitating then no longer,
'Sir,' I said, 'or Madam, truly your forgiveness I implore;
But the fact is I was napping, and so gently you came rapping,
And so faintly you came tapping, tapping at my chamber door,
That I scarce was sure I heard you' – here I opened wide the door; –
        Darkness there and nothing more.

Deep into that darkness peering, long I stood there wondering, fearing,
Doubting, dreaming dreams no mortal ever dared to dream before;
But the silence was unbroken, and the stillness gave no token,
And the only word there spoken was the whispered word, 'Lenore!'
This I whispered, and an echo murmured back the word 'Lenore!'
　　　Merely this and nothing more.

Back into the chamber turning, all my soul within me burning,
Soon again I heard the tapping somewhat louder than before.
'Surely,' said I, 'surely that is someone at my window lattice;
Let me see, then, what thereat is, and this mystery explore –
Let my heart be still a moment and this mystery explore; –
　　　'Tis the wind and nothing more!'

Open here I flung the shutter, when, with many a flirt and flutter
In there stepped a stately Raven of the saintly days of yore.
Not the least obeisance made he; not a minute stopped or stayed he;
But, with mien of lord or lady, perched above my chamber door –
Perched upon a bust of Pallas just above my chamber door –
　　　Perched, and sat, and nothing more.

Then this ebony bird beguiling my sad fancy into smiling,
By the grave and stern decorum of the countenance it wore,
'Thou thy crest be shorn and shaven, thou,' I said, 'are sure no craven,
Ghastly grim and ancient Raven wandering from the Nightly shore –
Tell me what thy lordly name is on the Night's Plutonian shore!'
　　　Quoth the Raven, 'Nevernore.'

Edgar Allan Poe (1809–1849)

Spring's Bedfellow

Spring went about the woods to-day,
The soft-foot winter-thief,
And found where idle sorrow lay
'Twixt flower and faded leaf.

She looked on him, and found him fair
For all she had been told;
She knelt adown beside him there,
And sang of days of old.

His open eyes beheld her nought,
Yet 'gan his lips to move;
But life and deeds were in her thought,
And he would sing of love.

So sang they till their eyes did meet,
And faded fear and shame;
More bold he grew, and she more sweet,
Until they sang the same.

Until, say they who know the thing,
Their very lips did kiss,
And Sorrow laid abed with Spring
Begat an earthly bliss.

William Morris (1834–1896)

The Violet

The violet in her greenwood bower,
    Where birchen boughs with hazels mingle,
May boast itself the fairest flower
    In glen, or copse, or forest dingle.

Though fair her gems of azure hue,
    Beneath the dewdrop's weight reclining;
I've seen an eye of lovelier blue,
    More sweet through wa'try lustre shining.

The summer sun that dew shall dry,
    Ere yet the day be past its morrow;
Nor longer in my false love's eye
    Remain'd the tear of parting sorrow.

Sir Walter Scott (1771–1832)

The Donkey

When fishes flew and forests walked
    And figs grew upon thorn,
Some moment when the moon was blood
    Then surely I was born.

With monstrous head and sickening cry
    And ears like errant wings,
The devil's walking parody
    On all four-footed things.

The tattered outlaw of the earth,
    Of ancient crooked will;
Starve, scourge, deride me: I am dumb,
    I keep my secret still.

Fools! For I also had my hour;
    One far fierce hour and sweet:
There was a shout about my ears,
    And palms before my feet.

G. K. Chesterton (1874–1936)

The Primrose

Upon this Primrose hill,
　Where, if Heav'n would distill
A shoure of raine, each severall drop might goe
To his owne primrose, and grow Manna so;
And where their forme, and their infinitie
　Make a terrestriall Galaxie,
　As the small starres doe in the skie:
I walke to finde a true Love; and I see
That 'tis not a mere woman, that is shee,
But must, or more, or lesse than woman bee.

Yet know I not, which flower
　I wish; a sixe, or foure;
For should my true-Love lesse than woman bee,
She were scarce any thing; and then, should she
Be more than woman, shee would get above
　All thought of sexe, and thinke to move
　My heart to study her, and not to love;
Both these were monsters; Since there must reside
Falsehood in woman, I could more abide,
She were by art, than Nature falsify'd.

Live Primrose then, and thrive
With thy true number five;
And woman, whom this flower doth represent,
With this mysterious number be content;
Ten is the farthest number; if halfe ten
Belong unto each woman, then
Each woman may take halfe us men,
Or if this will not serve their turne, Since all
Numbers are odde or even, and they fall
First into this, five, women may take us all.

John Donne (1572–1631)

In the Fields

Lord, when I look at lovely things which pass,
    Under old trees the shadows of young leaves
Dancing to please the wind along the grass,
    Or the gold stillness of the August sun on the August sheaves;
Can I believe there is a heavenlier world than this?
    And if there is
Will the strange heart of any everlasting thing
    Bring me these dreams that take my breath away?
They come at evening with the home-flying rooks and the scent of hay,
    Over the fields they come. They come in Spring.

Charlotte Mew (1869–1928)

APRIL

Dancing in the Breeze

There was an old Man with a Beard

There was an old Man with a beard,
Who said, 'It is just as I feared! –
Two Owls and a Hen, four Larks and a Wren,
Have all made their nests in my beard!'

Edward Lear (1812–1888)

General Prologue

FROM *THE CANTERBURY TALES*, LINES 1–18

Whan that Aprill with his shourés soote
The droghte of March hath perced to the roote,
And bathed every veyne in swich licour
Of which vertu engendred is the flour;
Whan Zephirus eek with his sweeté breeth
Inspired hath in every holt and heeth
The tendre croppés, and the yongé sonne
Hath in the Ram his halvé cours yronne,
And smalé fowelés maken melodye,
That slepen al the nyght with open ye
(So priketh hem nature in hir corages);
Thanne longen folk to goon on pilgrimages,
And palmerés for to seken straunge strondes,
To ferné halwes, kowthe in sondry londes;
And specially from every shires ende
Of Engelond to Caunterbury they wende,
The hooly blisful martir for to seke,
That hem hath holpen whan that they were seeke.

Geoffrey Chaucer (c. 1343–1400)

Advice

Now, you two eyes, that have all night been sleeping,
Come into the meadows, where the lambs are leaping;
See how they start at every swallow's shadow
That darts across their faces and their meadow.
See how the blades spring upright, when the Sun
Takes off the weight of raindrops, one by one.
See how a shower, that freshened leaves of grass,
Can make that bird's voice fresher than it was.
See how the squirrels lash the quiet trees
Into a tempest, where there is no breeze!
Now, you two eyes, that have all night been sleeping,
Come into the meadows, where the lambs are leaping.

W. H. Davies (1871–1940)

The Loveliest of Trees

A SHROPSHIRE LAD, II

Loveliest of trees, the cherry now
Is hung with bloom along the bough,
And stands about the woodlands ride
Wearing white for Eastertide.

Now, of my threescore years and ten,
Twenty will not come again,
And take from seventy springs a score,
It only leaves me fifty more.

And since to look at things in bloom
Fifty springs are little room,
About the woodlands I will go
To see the cherry hung with snow.

A. E. Housman (1859–1936)

I Wandered Lonely as a Cloud

WRITTEN AT TOWN-END, GRASMERE

I wandered lonely as a cloud
That floats on high o'er vales and hills,
When all at once I saw a crowd,
A host, of golden daffodils;
Beside the lake, beneath the trees,
Fluttering and dancing in the breeze.

Continuous as the stars that shine
And twinkle on the milky way,
They stretched in never-ending line
Along the margin of the bay:
Ten thousand saw I at a glance,
Tossing their heads in sprightly dance.

The waves beside them danced; but they
Out-did the sparkling waves in glee:
A poet could not but be gay,
In such a jocund company:
I gazed – and gazed – but little thought
What wealth the show to me had brought:

For oft, when on my couch I lie
In vacant or in pensive mood,
They flash upon that inward eye
Which is the bliss of solitude;
And then my heart with pleasure fills,
And dances with the daffodils.

William Wordsworth (1770–1850)

I so Liked Spring

I so liked Spring last year
    Because you were here; –
        The thrushes too –
Because it was these you so liked to hear –
        I so liked you.

    This year's a different thing, –
        I'll not think of you.
But I'll like the Spring because it is simply Spring
        As the thrushes do.

Charlotte Mew (1869–1928)

The Cherry Trees

Out of the dusk of distant woods
All round the April skies
Blossom-white, the cherry trees
Like lovely apparitions rise,

Like spirits strange to this ill world,
White strangers from a world apart,
Like silent promises of peace,
Like hope that blossoms in the heart.

Laurence Binyon (1869–1943)

I heard a Linnet Courting

I heard a linnet courting
　　His lady in the spring:
His mates were idly sporting,
　　Nor stayed to hear him sing
　　　　His song of love. –
I fear my speech distorting
　　　　His tender love.

The phrases of his pleading
　　Were full of young delight;
And she that gave him heeding
　　Interpreted aright
　　　　His gay, sweet notes, –
So sadly marred in the reading, –
　　　　His tender notes.

And when he ceased, the hearer
　　Awaited the refrain,
Till swiftly perching nearer
　　He sang his song again,
　　　　His pretty song: –
Would that my verse spake clearer
　　　　His tender song!

Ye happy, airy creatures!
　　That in the merry spring
Think not of what misfeatures
　　Or cares the year may bring;
　　　　But unto love
Resign your simple natures,
　　　　To tender love.

Robert Bridges (1844–1930)

Turquoise

when, as a child, I did wonder:
does it rain upon the ocean?
little did I know that this was mere foundation,
a prelude

to years spent trawling greater fathoms
– delving further from the raindrops –
perceiving caverns, uncharted, lit in emerald
and turquoise.

Joel Knight (1975–)

His Mansion the Pool

His Mansion in the Pool
The Frog forsakes –
He rises on a Log
And statements makes –
His Auditors two Worlds
Deducting me –
The Orator of April
Is hoarse Today –
His Mittens at his Feet
No Hand hath he –
His eloquence a Bubble
As Fame should be –
Applaud him to discover
To your chagrin
Demosthenes has vanished
In Waters Green –

Emily Dickinson (1830–1886)

Now fades the last long streak of snow

FROM *IN MEMORIAM A. H. H.*

Now fades the last long streak of snow
    Now burgeons every maze of quick
    About the flowering squares, and thick
By ashen roots the violets blow.

Now rings the woodland loud and long,
    The distance takes a lovelier hue,
    And drown'd in yonder living blue
The lark becomes a sightless song.

Now dance the lights on lawn and lea,
    The flocks are whiter down the vale,
    And milkier every milky sail
On winding stream or distant sea;

Where now the seamew pipes, or dives
    In yonder greening gleam, and fly
    The happy birds, that change their sky
To build and brood; that live their lives

From land to land; and in my breast
    Spring wakens too; and my regret
    Becomes an April violet,
And buds and blossoms like the rest.

Alfred, Lord Tennyson (1809–1892)

The Lent Lily

A SHROPSHIRE LAD, XXIX

'Tis spring; come out to ramble
    The hilly brakes around,
For under thorn and bramble
    About the hollow ground
    The primroses are found.

And there's the windflower chilly
    With all the winds at play,
And there's the Lenten lily
    That has not long to stay
    And dies on Easter day.

And since till girls go maying
    You find the primrose still,
And find the windflower playing
    With every wind at will,
    But not the daffodil,

Bring baskets now, and sally
    Upon the spring's array,
And bear from hill and valley
    The daffodil away
    That dies on Easter day.

A. E. Housman (1859–1936)

The Anglers Wish

I in these flowry Meads wou'd be:
These Chrystal streams should solace me:
To whose harmonious bubling noise,
I with my Angle wo'd rejoice
Sit here and see the *Turtle-Dove*,
Court his chaste Mate to acts of love,
Or on that bank, feel the west wind
Breath health and plenty, please my mind
To see sweet dew-drops kiss these flowers,
And then, washt off by *April*-showers:
Here hear my *Kenna* sing a song,
There see a Black-bird feed her young,
Or a *Leverock* build her nest;
Here, give my weary spirits rest,
And raise my low pitcht thoughts above
Earth, or what poor mortals love:
 Thus free from *Law-suits*, and the noise
 Of Princes Courts I wou'd rejoyce.

Or with my *Bryan*, and a book,
Loyter long days near *Shawford-brook*;
There sit by him, and eat my meat,
There see the Sun both rise and set:
There bid good morning to next day,
There meditate my time away:
 And angle on, and beg to have
 A quiet passage to a welcome grave.

Izaak Walton (1593–1683)

Folk Song

The cuckoo she's a pretty bird,
She sings as she flies,
She brings us good tidings,
She tells us no lies;
She sucketh white flowers
For to make her voice clear,
And the more she sings 'cuckoo!'
The summer draws near.

Anon

The Peaceful Western Wind

FROM *TWO BOOKES OF AYRES*, BOOK 2, CANTUS XII

1

The peacefull westerne winde
The winter stormes hath tam'd,
And nature in each kinde
The kinde heat hath inflam'd.
The forward buds so sweetly breathe
Out of their earthy bowers,
That heav'n which viewes their pompe beneath
Would faine be deckt with flowers.

2

See how the morning smiles
On her bright easterne hill,
And with soft steps beguiles
Them that lie slumbring still.
The musicke-loving birds are come
From cliffes and rockes unknowne,
To see the trees and briers blome
That late were over-flowne.

3

What Saturne did destroy,
Loves Queene revives againe;
And now her naked boy
Doth in the fields remaine:
Where he such pleasing change doth view
In ev'ry living thing,
As if the world were borne anew
To gratifie the Spring.

4

If all things life present,
Why die my comforts then?
Why suffers my content?
Am I the worst of men?
O, beautie, be not thou accus'd
Too justly in this case:
Unkindly if true love be us'd,
'Twill yeeld thee little grace.

Thomas Campion (1567–1620)

A Frisky Lamb

A frisky lamb
And a frisky child
Playing their pranks
   In a cowslip meadow:
The sky all blue
And the air all mild
And the fields all sun
   And the lanes half shadow.

Christina Rossetti (1830–1894)

The Hollow Wood

Out in the sun the goldfinch flits
Along the thistle-tops, flits and twits
Above the hollow wood
Where birds swim like fish –
Fish that laugh and shriek –
To and fro, far below
In the pale hollow wood.

Lichen, ivy, and moss
Keep evergreen the trees
That stand half-flayed and dying,
And the dead trees on their knees
In dog's-mercury and moss:
And the bright twit of the goldfinch drops
Down there as he flits on thistle-tops.

Edward Thomas (1878–1917)

Wood Anemonie

The wood anemonie through dead oak leaves
And in the thickest woods now blooms anew
And where the green briar, and the bramble weaves
Thick clumps o'green, anemonies thicker grew
And weeping flowers, in thousands pearled in dew
People the woods and brakes, hid hollows there
White, yellow and purple hued the wide wood through
What pretty, drooping weeping flowers they are
The clipt-frilled leaves the slender stalk they bear
On which the drooping flower hangs weeping dew
How beautiful through april time and may
The woods look, filled with wild anemonie
And every little spinney now looks gay
With flowers mid brushwood and the huge oak tree.

John Clare (1793–1864)

The Silk Worm

TRANSLATED BY WILLIAM COWPER

The beams of April, ere it goes,
A worm, scarce visible, disclose;
All winter long content to dwell
The tenant of his native shell.
The same prolific season gives
The sustenance by which he lives,
The mulb'ry-leaf, a simple store,
That serves him – till he needs no more!
For, his dimensions once complete,
Thenceforth none ever sees him eat;
Tho' till his growing time be past,
Scarce ever is he seen to fast.
That hour arriv'd, his work begins.
He spins and weaves, and weaves and spins;
Till circle upon circle wound
Careless around him and around,
Conceals him with a veil, tho' slight,
Impervious to the keenest sight.
Thus self-enclos'd, as in a cask,
At length he finishes his task;
And, tho' a worm, when he was lost,
Or caterpillar at the most,
When next we see him, wings he wears,
And in papilio-pomp appears;
Becomes oviparous; supplies,
With future worms and future flies,
The next-ensuing year; – and dies!

Well were it for the world, if all
Who creep about this earthly ball,
Though shorter-liv'd than most he be,
Were useful in their kind as he.

Vincent Bourne (1695–1747)

April Rise

If ever I saw blessing in the air
    I see it now in this still early day
Where lemon-green the vaporous morning drips
    Wet sunlight on the powder of my eye.

Blown bubble-film of blue, the sky wraps round
    Weeds of warm light whose every root and rod
Splutters with soapy green, and all the world
    Sweats with the bead of summer in its bud.

If ever I heard blessing it is there
    Where birds in trees that shoals and shadows are
Splash with their hidden wings and drops of sound
    Break on my ears their crests of throbbing air.

Pure in the haze the emerald sun dilates,
    The lips of sparrows milk the mossy stones,
While white as water by the lake a girl
    Swims her green hand among the gathered swans.

Now, as the almond burns its smoking wick,
    Dropping small flames to light the candled grass;
Now, as my low blood scales its second chance,
    If ever world were blessed, now it is.

Laurie Lee (1914–1997)

To Blossoms

Faire pledges of a fruitfull Tree,
    Why do yee fall so fast?
    Your date is not so past,
But you may stay yet here a while,
    To blush and gently smile;
       And go at last.

What, were yee born to be
    An houre or half's delight;
    And so to bid goodnight?
'Twas pitie Nature brought yee forth,
    Meerly to shew your worth,
       And lose you quite.

But you are lovely Leaves, where we
    May read how soon things have
    Their end, though ne'er so brave:
And after they have shown their pride,
    Like you, a-while: They glide
       Into the Grave.

Robert Herrick (1591–1674)

The ascent of the lark

The ascent of the lark is invisible mending

Ian Hamilton Finlay (1925–2006)

Home Thoughts from Abroad

I

Oh, to be in England
Now that April's there,
And whoever wakes in England
Sees, some morning, unaware,
That the lowest boughs and brushwood sheaf
Round the elm-tree bole are in tiny leaf,
While the chaffinch sings on the orchard bough
In England – now!

II

And after April, when May follows,
And the whitethroat builds, and all the swallows!
Hark, where my blossomed pear-tree in the hedge
Leans to the field and scatters on the clover
Blossoms and dewdrops – at the bent spray's edge –
That's the wise thrush; he sings each song twice over,
Lest you should think he never could recapture
The first fine careless rapture!
And though the fields look rough with hoary dew
All will be gay when noontide wakes anew
The buttercups, the little children's dower
 – Far brighter than this gaudy melon-flower!

Robert Browning (1812–1889)

Spring

Frost-locked all the winter,
Seeds, and roots, and stones of fruits,
What shall make their sap ascend
That they may put forth shoots?
Tips of tender green,
Leaf, or blade, or sheath;
Telling of the hidden life
That breaks forth underneath,
Life nursed in its grave by Death.

Blows the thaw-wind pleasantly,
Drips the soaking rain,
By fits looks down the waking sun:
Young grass springs on the plain;
Young leaves clothe early hedgerow trees;
Seeds, and roots, and stones of fruits,
Swollen with sap put forth their shoots;
Curled-headed ferns sprout in the lane;
Birds sing and pair again.

There is no time like Spring,
When life's alive in everything,
Before new nestlings sing,
Before cleft swallows speed their journey back
Along the trackless track –
God guides their wing,
He spreads their table that they nothing lack, –
Before the daisy grows a common flower
Before the sun has power
To scorch the world up in his noontide hour.

There is no time like Spring,
Like Spring that passes by;
There is no life like Spring-life born to die, –
Piercing the sod,
Clothing the uncouth clod,
Hatched in the nest,
Fledged on the windy bough,
Strong on the wing:
There is no time like Spring that passes by,
Now newly born, and now
Hastening to die.

Christina Rossetti (1830–1894)

The Babbling Brook

FROM *THE BROOK, AN IDYLL*

I come from haunts of coot and hern,
    I make a sudden sally
And sparkle out among the fern,
    To bicker down a valley.

By thirty hills I hurry down
    Or slip between the ridges,
By twenty thorps, a little town
    And half a hundred bridges.

Till last by Philip's farm I flow
    To join the brimming river,
For men may come and men may go
    But I go on for ever.

I chatter over stony ways
    In little sharps and trebles,
I bubble into eddying bays,
    I babble on the pebbles.

With many a curve my banks I fret
    By many a field and fallow,
And many a fairy foreland set
With willow-weed and mallow.

I chatter, chatter, as I flow
    To join the brimming river,
For men may come and men may go
    But I go on for ever.

I wind about, and in and out,
    With here a blossom sailing,
And here and there a lusty trout,
    And here and there a grayling,

And here and there a foamy flake
    Upon me, as I travel
With many a silvery waterbreak
    Above the golden gravel,

And draw them all along, and flow
    To join the brimming river
For men may come and men may go
    But I go on for ever.

Alfred, Lord Tennyson (1809–1892)

Birds Nests

How fresh the air the birds how busy now
In every walk if I but peep I find
Nests newly made or finished all and lined
With hair and thistle down and in the bough
Of little awthorn huddled up in green
The leaves still thickening as the spring gets age
The Pinks quite round and snug and closely laid
And linnets of materials loose and rough
And still hedge sparrow moping in the shade
Near the hedge bottom weaves of homely stuff
Dead grass and mosses green an hermitage
For secresy and shelter rightly made
And beautiful it is to walk beside
The lanes and hedges where their homes abide.

John Clare (1793–1864)

Spring

Spring, the sweet spring, is the year's pleasant king;
Then blooms each thing, then maids dance in a ring,
Cold doth not sting, the pretty birds do sing:
    Cuckoo, jug-jug, pu-we, to-witta-woo!

The palm and may make country houses gay,
Lambs frisk and play, the shepherds pipe all day,
And we hear aye birds tune this merry lay:
    Cuckoo, jug-jug, pu-we, to-witta-woo!

The fields breathe sweet, the daisies kiss our feet,
Young lovers meet, old wives a-sunning sit;
In every street these tunes our ears do greet:
    Cuckoo, jug-jug, pu-we, to-witta-woo!
        Spring, the sweet spring.

Thomas Nashe (1567–c. 1601)

Proud Songsters

The thrushes sing as the sun is going,
And the finches whistle in ones and pairs,
And as it gets dark loud nightingales
      In bushes
Pipe, as they can when April wears,
   As if all Time were theirs.

These are brand-new birds of twelve-months' growing,
Which a year ago, or less than twain,
No finches were, nor nightingales,
      Nor thrushes,
But only particles of grain,
   And earth, and air, and rain.

Thomas Hardy (1840–1928)

The Nightingale

The nightingale, as soon as April bringeth
Unto her rested sense a perfect waking,
While late bare earth, proud of new clothing, springeth,
Sings out her woes, a thorn her song-book making,
    And mournfully bewailing,
    Her throat in tunes expresseth
    What grief her breast oppresseth
    For Tereus' force on her chaste will prevailing
        O Philomela fair, O take some gladness,
        That here is juster cause of plaintful sadness:
        Thine earth now springs, mine fadeth;
        Thy thorn without, my thorn my heart invadeth.

Alas, she hath no other cause of anguish
But Tereus' love, on her by strong hand wroken,
Wherein she suffering, all her spirits' languish;
Full womanlike complains her will was broken.
    But I, who daily craving,
    Cannot have to content me,
    Have more cause to lament me,
    Since wanting is more woe than too much having.
        O Philomela fair, O take some gladness,
        That here is juster cause of plaintful sadness:
        Thine earth now springs, mine fadeth;
        Thy thorn without, my thorn my heart invadeth.

Sir Philip Sidney (1554–1586)

Water Colours

The trembling water glimpsed through dark tangle
Of late-month April's delicatest thorn,
One moment put the cuckoo-flower to scorn
Where its head hangs by sedges, Severn bank-full.
But dark water has a hundred fires on it;
As the sky changes it changes and ranges through
Sky colours and thorn colours, and more would do,
Were not the blossom truth so quick on it,
And beauty brief in action as first dew.

Ivor Gurney (1890–1937)

MAY

A Thousand Fragrant Posies

Song on May Morning

Now the bright morning star, Day's harbinger,
Comes dancing from the east, and leads with her
The flowery May, who from her green lap throws
The yellow cowslip and the pale primrose.
    Hail, bounteous May, that dost inspire
    Mirth, and youth, and warm desire!
    Woods and groves are of thy dressing;
Hill and dale doth boast thy blessing.
Thus we salute thee with our early song,
And welcome thee, and wish thee long.

John Milton (1608–1674)

Spring Goeth All in White

Spring goeth all in white,
Crowned with milk-white may:
In fleecy flocks of light
O'er heaven the white clouds stray:

White butterflies in the air;
White daisies prank the ground:
The cherry and hoary pear
Scatter their snow around.

Robert Bridges (1844–1930)

May Song

Birds in the green of my garden,
    Blackbirds and throstle and wren,
Wet your dear wings in the tears that are Spring's,
    And so to your singing again!
Birds in my blossoming orchard,
    Chaffinch and goldfinch and lark,
Preen your bright wings, little happy live things;
    The May trees grow white in the park!

Birds in the leafy wet woodlands,
    Cuckoo and nightingale brown,
Sing to the sound of rain on green ground –
    The rain on green leaves dripping down!
Fresh with the rain of the May-time,
    Rich with the promise of June,
Deep in her heart, where the little leaves part,
    Love, like a bird, sings in tune!

E. Nesbit (1858–1924)

Maye

FROM *MAYE, THE SHEPHAERDES CALENDER*, LINES 1–16

Is not thilke the mery month of May,
When love lads masken in fresh aray?
How falles it then, we no merrier bene,
Ylike as others, girt in gawdy greene?
Our bloncket liveryes bene all to sadde,
For thilke same season, when all is ycladd
With pleasaunce: the grownd with grasse, the Woods
With greene leaves, the bushes with bloosoming Buds.
Yougthes folke now flocken in every where,
To gather may buskets and smelling brere:
And home they hasten the postes to dight,
And all the Kirke pillours eare day light,
With Hawthorne buds, and swete Eglantine,
And girlonds of roses and Sopps in wine.
Such merimake holy Saints doth queme,
But we here sytten as drowned in a dreme.

Edmund Spenser (c. 1552–1599)

Spring

FROM *LOVE'S LABOUR'S LOST*, ACT V SCENE II

When daisies pied and violets blue,
    And lady-smocks, all silver-white,
And cuckoo-buds of yellow hue
    Do paint the meadows with delight,
The cuckoo then on every tree
Mocks married men, for thus sings he: Cuckoo!
Cuckoo, cuckoo – O word of fear,
Unpleasing to a married ear.

When shepherds pipe on oaten straws,
    And merry larks are ploughmen's clocks;
When turtles tread, and rooks and daws,
    And maidens bleach their summer smocks,
The cuckoo then on every tree
Mocks married men, for thus sings he: Cuckoo!
Cuckoo, cuckoo – O word of fear,
Unpleasing to a married ear.

William Shakespeare (1564–1616)

To a Sky-Lark

WRITTEN AT RYDAL MOUNT

Ethereal minstrel! pilgrim of the sky!
Dost thou despise the earth where cares abound?
Or, while the wings aspire, are heart and eye
Both with thy nest upon the dewy ground?
Thy nest which thou canst drop into at will,
Those quivering wings composed, that music still!

Leave to the nightingale her shady wood;
A privacy of glorious light is thine;
Whence thou dost pour upon the world a flood
Of harmony, with instinct more divine;
Type of the wise who soar, but never roam;
True to the kindred points of Heaven and Home!

William Wordsworth (1770–1850)

Sonnet

After dark vapors have oppress'd our plains
    For a long dreary season, comes a day
    Born of the gentle South, and clears away
From the sick heavens all unseemly stains.
The anxious month, relieved of its pains,
    Takes as a long-lost right the feel of May;
    The eyelids with the passing coolness play
Like rose leaves with the drip of Summer rains.
The calmest thoughts came round us; as of leaves
    Budding – fruit ripening in stillness – Autumn suns
Smiling at eve upon the quiet sheaves –
Sweet Sappho's cheek – a smiling infant's breath –
    The gradual sand that through an hour-glass runs –
A woodland rivulet – a Poet's death.

John Keats (1795–1821)

The Passionate Shepherd to his Love

Come live with me and be my love,
And we will all the pleasures prove,
That hills and valleys, dales and fields,
And all the craggy mountains yields.

There we will sit upon the rocks,
And see the shepherds feed their flocks,
By shallow rivers to whose falls
Melodious birds sing madrigals.

And I will make thee beds of roses
With a thousand fragrant posies,
A cap of flowers, and a kirtle,
Embroidered all with leaves of myrtle;

A gown made of the finest wool
Which from our pretty lambs we pull;
Fair lined slippers for the cold,
With buckles of the purest gold;

A belt of straw and ivy-buds,
With coral clasps and amber studs:
And if these pleasures may thee move,
Come live with me and be my love.

Thy silver dishes for thy meat
As precious as the gods do eat,
Shall on an ivory table be
Prepared each day for thee and me.

The shepherds' swains shall dance and sing
For thy delight each May morning:
If these delights thy mind may move,
Then live with me and be my love.

Christopher Marlowe (1564–1593)

Spring

Nothing is so beautiful as Spring –
    When weeds, in wheels, shoot long and lovely and lush;
    Thrush's eggs look little low heavens, and thrush
Through the echoing timber does so rinse and wring
The ear, it strikes like lightnings to hear him sing;
    The glassy peartree leaves and blooms, they brush
    The descending blue; that blue is all in a rush
With richness; the racing lambs too have fair their fling.

What is all this juice and all this joy?
    A strain of the earth's sweet being in the beginning
In Eden garden. – Have, get, before it cloy,
    Before it cloud, Christ, lord, and sour with sinning,
Innocent mind and Mayday in girl and boy,
    Most, O maid's child, thy choice and worthy the winning.

Gerard Manley Hopkins (1844–1889)

Sheep in the Cotswolds

FROM *POLY-OLBION*

And, now that everything may in the proper place
Most aptly be contriv'd, the sheep our Wold doth breed
(The simplest though it seem) shall our description need,
And shepherd-like, the Muse thus of that kind doth speak:
No brown, nor sullied black the face or legs doth streak,
Like those of Moreland, Cank, or of the Cambrian Hills
That lightly laden are: but Cotswold wisely fills
Her with the whitest kind: whose brows so woolly be,
As men in her fair sheep no emptiness should see.
The staple deep and thick, through, to the very grain,
Most strongly keepeth out the violentest rain:
A body long and large, the buttocks equal broad;
As fit to undergo the full and weighty load.
And of the fleecy face, the flank doth nothing lack,
But everywhere is stor'd; the belly, as the back.
The fair and goodly flock, the shepherd's only pride,
As white as winter's snow, when from the river's side
He drives his new-wash'd sheep; or on the shearing-day,
When as the lusty ram, with those rich spoils of May
His crooked horns hath crown'd; the bell-wether, so brave
As none in all the flock they like themselves would have.

Michael Drayton (1563–1631)

Bounty

The full woods overflow
    Among the meadow's gold!
A blue-bell wave has rolled
    Where crowded cowslips grow.
The drifting hawthorn snow
    Brims over hill and wold.
The full woods overflow
    Among the meadow's gold;
The ditches are aglow!
    The marshes cannot hold
Their kingcups manifold
    Heav'n's beauty crowds below,
The full woods overflow!

Mary Webb (1881–1927)

May

O! the month of May, the merry month of May,
    So frolic, so gay, and so green, so green, so green!
O! and then did I unto my true Love say,
    Sweet Peg, thou shalt be my Summer's Queen.

Now the nightingale, the pretty nightingale,
    The sweetest singer in all the forest's choir,
Entreats thee, sweet Peggy, to hear thy true Love's tale:
    Lo! yonder she sitteth, her breast against a briar.

But O! I spy the cuckoo, the cuckoo, the cuckoo;
    See where she sitteth; come away, my joy:
Come away, I prithee, I do not like the cuckoo
    Should sing where my Peggy and I kiss and toy.

O! the month of May, the merry month of May,
    So frolic, so gay, and so green, so green, so green!
And then did I unto my true Love say,
    Sweet Peg, thou shalt be my Summer's Queen.

Thomas Dekker (c. 1572–1632)

These Blushing Borders

FROM *SUMMER, THE SEASONS*

Along these blushing borders, bright with dew,
And in yon mingled wilderness of flowers,
Fair-handed Spring unbosoms every grace:
Throws out the snowdrop and the crocus first;
The daisy, primrose, violet darkly blue,
And polyanthus of unnumber'd dyes;
The yellow wallflower, stain'd with iron brown;
And lavish stock that scents the garden round:
From the soft wing of vernal breezes shed,
Anemonies, auriculas, enrich'd
With shining meal o'er all their velvet leaves:
And full ranunculus, of growing red.
Then comes the tulip race, where Beauty plays
Her idle freaks: from family diffused
To family, as flies the father-dust,
The varied colours run; and while they break
On the charm'd eye, the exulting florist marks,
With secret pride, the wonders of his hand.
No gradual bloom is wanting; from the bud,
First-born of Spring, to Summer's musky tribes:
Nor hyacinths, of purest virgin white,
Low-bent, and blushing inward; nor jonquils,
Of potent fragrance; nor narcissus fair,
As o'er the fabled fountain hanging still;
Nor broad carnations; nor gay spotted pinks;
Nor, shower'd from every bush, the damask rose;
Infinite numbers, delicacies, smells,
With hues on hues expression cannot paint,
The breath of Nature, and her endless bloom.

James Thomson (1700–1748)

Ode to a Nightingale

VERSES 1–4

I

My heart aches, and a drowsy numbness pains
    My sense, as though of hemlock I had drunk,
Or emptied some dull opiate to the drains
    One minute past, and Lethe-wards had sunk:
'Tis not through envy of thy happy lot,
    But being too happy in thine happiness, –
        That thou, light-winged Dryad of the trees,
            In some melodious plot
Of beechen green, and shadows numberless,
    Singest of summer in full-throated ease.

II

O, for a draught of vintage! that hath been
    Cool'd a long age in the deep-delved earth,
Tasting of Flora and the country green,
    Dance, and Provençal song, and sunburnt mirth!
O for a beaker full of the warm South,
    Full of the true, the blushful Hippocrene,
        With beaded bubbles winking at the brim,
            And purple-stained mouth;
That I might drink, and leave the world unseen,
    And with thee fade away into the forest dim:

III

Fade far away, dissolve, and quite forget
    What thou among the leaves hast never known,
The weariness, the fever, and the fret
    Here, where men sit and hear each other groan;
Where palsy shakes a few, sad, last grey hairs,
      Where youth grows pale, and spectre-thin, and dies;
        Where but to think is to be full of sorrow
          And leaden-eyed despairs,
      Where Beauty cannot keep her lustrous eyes,
        Or new Love pine at them beyond to-morrow

IV

Away! away! for I will fly to thee,
    Not charioted by Bacchus and his pards,
But on the viewless wings of Poesy,
    Though the dull brain perplexes and retards:
Already with thee! tender is the night,
      And haply the Queen-Moon is on her throne,
        Cluster'd around by all her starry Fays;
          But here there is no light,
      Save what from heaven is with the breezes blown
        Through verdurous glooms and winding mossy ways.

John Keats (1795–1821)

Home Pictures in May

The sunshine bathes in clouds of many hues
And mornings feet are gemmed with early dews
Warm Daffodils about the garden beds
Peep thro their pale slim leaves their golden heads
Sweet earthly suns of spring – the Gosling broods
In coats of sunny green about the road
Waddle in extacy – and in rich moods
The old hen leads her flickering chicks abroad
Oft scuttling neath her wings to see the kite
Hang waving oer them in the springs blue light
The sparrows round their new nests chirp with glee
And sweet the Robin springs young luxury shares
Tuteling its song in feathery Gooseberry tree
While watching worms the Gardeners spade unbears.

John Clare (1793–1864)

To a Butterfly

WRITTEN IN THE ORCHARD, TOWN-END, GRASMERE

STAY near me – do not take thy flight!
A little longer stay in sight!
Much converse do I find in thee,
Historian of my infancy!
Float near me; do not yet depart!
Dead times revive in thee:
Thou bring'st, gay creature as thou art!
A solemn image to my heart,
My father's family!

Oh! pleasant, pleasant were the days,
The time, when, in our childish plays,
My sister Emmeline and I
Together chased the butterfly!
A very hunter did I rush
Upon the prey: – with leaps and springs
I followed on from brake to bush;
But she, God love her, feared to brush
The dust from off its wings.

William Wordsworth (1770–1850)

Two Pewits

Under the after-sunset sky
Two pewits sport and cry,
More white than is the moon on high
Riding the dark surge silently;
More black than earth. Their cry
Is the one sound under the sky.
They alone move, now low, now high,
And merrily they cry
To the mischievous Spring sky,
Plunging earthward, tossing high,
Over the ghost who wonders why
So merrily they cry and fly,
Nor choose 'twixt earth and sky,
While the moon's quarter silently
Rides, and earth rests as silently.

Edward Thomas (1878–1917)

Dandelions

Incorrigible, brash,
They brighten the cinder path of my childhood,
Unsubtle, the opposite of primroses,
But, unlike primroses, capable
Of growing anywhere, railway track, pierhead,
Like our extrovert friends who never
Make us fall in love, yet fill
The primroseless roseless gaps.

Louis MacNeice (1907–1963)

The Song of Wandering Aengus

I went out to the hazel wood,
Because a fire was in my head,
And cut and peeled a hazel wand,
And hooked a berry to a thread;
And when white moths were on the wing,
And moth-like stars were flickering out,
I dropped the berry in a stream
And caught a little silver trout.

When I had laid it on the floor
I went to blow the fire aflame,
But something rustled on the floor,
And someone called me by my name:
It had become a glimmering girl
With apple blossom in her hair
Who called me by my name and ran
And faded through the brightening air.

Though I am old with wandering
Through hollow lands and hilly lands,
I will find out where she has gone,
And kiss her lips and take her hands;
And walk among long dappled grass,
And pluck till time and times are done,
The silver apples of the moon,
The golden apples of the sun.

W. B. Yeats (1865–1939)

The Starlight Night

Look at the stars! look, look up at the skies!
  O look at all the fire-folk sitting in the air!
  The bright boroughs, the circle-citadels there!
Down in dim woods the diamond delves! the elves'-eyes!
The grey lawns cold where gold, where quickgold lies!
  Wind-beat whitebeam! airy abeles set on a flare!
  Flake-doves sent floating forth at a farmyard scare!
Ah well! it is all a purchase, all is a prize.

Buy then! bid then! – What? – Prayer, patience, alms, vows.
Look, look: a May-mess, like on orchard boughs!
  Look! March-bloom, like on mealed-with-yellow sallows!
These are indeed the barn; withindoors house
The shocks. This piece-bright paling shuts the spouse
  Christ home, Christ and his mother and all his hallows.

Gerard Manley Hopkins (1844–1889)

A Bed of Forget-me-nots

Is love so prone to change and rot
We are fain to rear forget-me-not
By measure in a garden plot? –

I love its growth at large and free
By untrod path and unlopped tree,
Or nodding by the unpruned hedge,
Or on the water's dangerous edge
Where flags and meadowsweet blow rank
With rushes on the quaking bank.

Love is not taught in learning's school,
Love is not parcelled out by rule;
Hath curb or call an answer got? –
So free must be forget-me-not.
Give me the flame no dampness dulls,
The passion of the instinctive pulse,
Love steadfast as a fixèd star,
Tender as doves with nestlings are,
More large than time, more strong than death:
This all creation travails of –
She groans not for a passing breath –
This is forget-me-not and love.

Christina Rossetti (1830–1894)

By Severn

If England, her spirit lives anywhere
It is by Severn, by hawthorns and grand willows
Earth heaves up twice a hundred feet in air
And ruddy clay-falls scooped out to the weedy shallows.
There in the brakes of May spring has her chambers,
Robing-rooms of hawthorn, cowslip, cuckoo flower –
Wonder complete changes for each square joy's hour,
Past thought miracles are there and beyond numbers.
If for the drab atmospheres and managed lighting
In London town, Oriana's playwrights had
Wainlode her theatre and then coppice-clad
Hill for her ground of sauntering and idle waiting,
Why, then I think, our chiefest glory of pride
(The Elizabethans of Thames, south and northern side)
Would nothing of its meeting be denied,
And her sons praises from England's mouth again be outcried.

Ivor Gurney (1890–1937)

The Glory

The glory of the beauty of the morning, –
The cuckoo crying over the untouched dew;
The blackbird that has found it, and the dove
That tempts me on to something sweeter than love;
White clouds ranged even and fair as new-mown hay;
The heat, the stir, the sublime vacancy
Of sky and meadow and forest and my own heart: –
The glory invites me, yet it leaves me scorning
All I can ever do, all I can be,
Beside the lovely of motion, shape, and hue,
The happiness I fancy fit to dwell
In beauty's presence. Shall I now this day
Begin to seek as far as heaven, as hell,
Wisdom or strength to match this beauty, start
And tread the pale dust pitted with small dark drops,
In hope to find whatever it is I seek,
Hearkening to short-lived happy-seeming things
That we know naught of, in the hazel copse?
Or must I be content with discontent
As larks and swallows are perhaps with wings?
And shall I ask at the day's end once more
What beauty is, and what I can have meant
By happiness? And shall I let all go,
Glad, weary, or both? Or shall I perhaps know
That I was happy oft and oft before,
Awhile forgetting how I am fast pent,
How dreary-swift, with naught to travel to,
Is Time? I cannot bite the day to the core.

Edward Thomas (1878–1917)

The Spring

Now that the Winter's gone, the earth hath lost
Her snow-white robes, and now no more the frost
Candies the grass, or casts an icy cream
Upon the silver lake or crystal stream;
But the warm sun thaws the benumbed earth,
And makes it tender; gives a sacred birth
To the dead swallow; wakes in hollow tree
The drowsy cuckoo, and the humble-bee.
Now do a choir of chirping minstrels bring
In triumph to the world, the youthful Spring.
The valleys, hills, and woods in rich array
Welcome the coming of the long'd for May.
Now all things smile, only my Love doth lour;
Nor hath the scalding noonday sun the power
To melt that marble ice, which still doth hold
Her heart congealed, and makes her pity cold.
The ox, which lately did for shelter fly
Into the stall, doth now securely lie
In open fields; and love no more is made
By the fireside, but in the cooler shade
Amyntas now doth with his Chloris sleep
Under a sycamore, and all things keep
Time with the season; only she doth carry
June in her eyes, in her heart January.

Thomas Carew (1594/5–1640)

The Flowering May-thorn Tree

FROM *ALICE DU CLOS*

There stands the flow'ring may-thorn tree!
From thro' the veiling mist you see
    The black and shadowy stem; –
Smit by the sun the mist in glee
Dissolves to lightsome jewelry –
    Each blossom hath its gem!

Samuel Taylor Coleridge (1772–1834)

May

When May is in his prime, then may each heart rejoice;
When May bedecks each branch with green, each bird strains forth his
    voice.
The lively sap creeps up into the blooming thorn;
The flowers, which cold in prison kept, now laugh the frost to scorn.
All nature's imps triumph whiles joyful May doth last;
When May is gone, of all the year the pleasant time is past.

May makes the cheerful hue, May breeds and brings new blood;
May marcheth throughout every limb, May makes the merry mood.
May pricketh tender hearts their warbling notes to tune;
Full strange it is, yet some we see do make their May in June.
Thus things are strangely wrought while joyful May doth last;
Take May in time, when May is gone the pleasant time is past.

All ye that live on earth, and have your May at will
Rejoice in May, as I do now, and use your May with skill.
Use May while that you may, for May hath but his time,
When all the fruit is gone, it is too late the tree to climb.
Your liking and your lust is fresh while May doth last;
When May is gone, of all the year the pleasant time is past.

Richard Edwardes (1525–1566)

The Lilac is in Bloom

FROM *THE OLD VICARAGE, GRANTCHESTER*

(*Café des Westens, Berlin, May 1912*)

Just now the lilac is in bloom,
All before my little room;
And in my flower-beds, I think,
Smile the carnations and the pink;
And down the borders, well I know,
The poppy and the pansy blow ...
Oh! there the chestnuts, summer through,
Beside the river make for you
A tunnel of green gloom, and sleep
Deeply above; and green and deep
The stream mysterious glides beneath,
Green as a dream and deep as death.
 – Oh, damn! I know it! and I know
How the May fields all golden show,
And when the day is young and sweet,
Gild gloriously the bare feet
That run to bathe ...

Ah God! to see the branches stir
Across the moon at Grantchester!
To smell the thrilling-sweet and rotten
Unforgettable, unforgotten
River-smell, and hear the breeze
Sobbing in the little trees.
Say, do the elm-clumps greatly stand
Still guardians of that holy land?
The chestnuts shade, in reverend dream,
The yet unacademic stream?
Is dawn a secret shy and cold

Anadyomene, silver and gold?
And sunset still a golden sea
From Haslingfield to Madingley?
And after, ere the night is born,
Do hares come out about the corn?
Oh, is the water sweet and cool,
Gentle and brown, above the pool?
And laughs the immortal river still
Under the mill, under the mill?
Say, is there Beauty yet to find?
And Certainty? and Quiet kind?
Deep meadows yet, for to forget
The lies, and truths, and pain? ... oh! yet
Stands the Church clock at ten to three?
And is there honey still for tea?

Rupert Brooke (1887–1915)

Jabberwocky

'Twas brillig, and the slithy toves
    Did gyre and gimble in the wabe:
All mimsy were the borogoves,
    And the mome raths outgrabe.

'Beware the Jabberwock, my son!
    The jaws that bite, the claws that catch!
Beware the Jubjub bird, and shun
    The frumious Bandersnatch!'

He took his vorpal sword in hand;
    Long time the manxome foe he sought –
So rested he by the Tumtum tree
    And stood awhile in thought.

And, as in uffish thought he stood,
    The Jabberwock, with eyes of flame,
Came whiffling through the tulgey wood,
    And burbled as it came!

One, two! One, two! And through and through
    The vorpal blade went snicker-snack!
He left it dead, and with its head
    He went galumphing back.

'And hast thou slain the Jabberwock?
    Come to my arms, my beamish boy!
O frabjous day! Callooh! Callay!'
    He chortled in his joy.

'Twas brillig, and the slithy toves
    Did gyre and gimble in the wabe:
All mimsy were the borogoves,
    And the mome raths outgrabe.

Lewis Carroll (1832–1898)

The Cloud

LINES 1–44

I bring fresh showers for the thirsting flowers,
    From the seas and the streams;
I bear light shade for the leaves when laid
    In their noonday dreams.
From my wings are shaken the dews that waken
    The sweet buds every one,
When rocked to rest on their mother's breast,
    As she dances about the sun.
I wield the flail of the lashing hail,
    And whiten the green plains under,
And then again I dissolve it in rain,
    And laugh as I pass in thunder.

I sift the snow on the mountains below,
    And their great pines groan aghast;
And all the night 'tis my pillow white,
    While I sleep in the arms of the blast.
Sublime on the towers of my skiey bowers,
    Lightning my pilot sits;
In a cavern under is fettered the thunder,
    It struggles and howls at fits;
Over earth and ocean, with gentle motion,
    This pilot is guiding me,
Lured by the love of the genii that move
    In the depths of the purple sea;
Over the rills, and the crags, and the hills,
    Over the lakes and the plains,
Wherever he dream, under mountain or stream,
    The Spirit he loves remains;
And I all the while bask in Heaven's blue smile,

206

Whilst he is dissolving in rains.
The sanguine Sunrise, with his meteor eyes,
    And his burning plumes outspread,
Leaps on the back of my sailing rack,
    When the morning star shines dead;
As on the jag of a mountain crag,
    Which an earthquake rocks and swings,
An eagle alit one moment may sit
    In the light of its golden wings.
And when Sunset may breathe, from the lit sea beneath,
    Its ardours of rest and of love,
And the crimson pall of eve may fall
    From the depth of Heaven above,
With wings folded I rest, on mine aëry nest,
    As still as a brooding dove.

Percy Bysshe Shelley (1792–1822)

The Throstle

'Summer is coming, summer is coming.
　　I know it, I know it, I know it.
Light again, leaf again, life again, love again,'
　　Yes, my wild little Poet.

Sing the new year in under the blue.
　　Last year you sang it as gladly.
'New, new, new, new'! Is it then *so* new
　　That you should carol so madly?

'Love again, song again, nest again, young again,'
　　Never a prophet so crazy!
And hardly a daisy as yet, little friend,
　　See, there is hardly a daisy.

'Here again, here, here, here, happy year'
　　O warble unchidden, unbidden!
Summer is coming, is coming, my dear,
　　And all the winters are hidden.

Alfred, Lord Tennyson (1809–1892)

Sonnet Written at the Close of Spring

The garlands fade that Spring so lately wove
    Each simple flower, which she had nursed in dew,
Anemones that spangled every grove,
    The primrose wan, and harebell mildly blue.
No more shall violets linger in the dell,
    Or purple orchis variegate the plain,
Till Spring again shall call forth every bell,
    And dress with humid hands her wreaths again.
Ah! poor humanity! so frail, so fair,
    Are the fond visions of thy early day,
Till tyrant passion, and corrosive care
    Bid all thy fairy colours fade away!
Another May new buds and flowers shall bring;
Ah! why has happiness – no second Spring?

Charlotte Smith (1749–1806)

JUNE

The Cornfield Stretched a Tender Green

Summer is icumen in

Sumer is icumin in –
Lhude sing, cuccu!
Groweth sed and bloweth med
And springth the wude nu.
Sing, cuccu!

Awe bleteth after lomb,
Lhouth after calve cu,
Bulluc sterteth, bucke verteth.
Murie sing, cuccu!
Cuccu, cuccu,
Wel singes thu, cuccu!
Ne swik thu naver nu!

Sing, cuccu, nu! Sing, cuccu!
Sing, cuccu! Sing, cuccu, nu!

Anon (13th century)

Overlooking the River Stour

The swallows flew in the curves of an eight
    Above the river-gleam
    In the wet June's last beam:
Like little crossbows animate
The swallows flew in the curves of an eight
    Above the river-gleam.

Planing up shavings of crystal spray
    A moor-hen darted out
    From the bank thereabout,
And through the stream-shine ripped his way;
Planing up shavings of crystal spray
    A moor-hen darted out.

Closed were the kingcups; and the mead
    Dripped in monotonous green,
    Though the day's morning sheen
Had shown it golden and honeybee'd;
Closed were the kingcups; and the mead
    Dripped in monotonous green.

And never I turned my head, alack,
    While these things met my gaze
    Through the pane's drop-drenched glaze,
To see the more behind my back ...
O never I turned, but let, alack,
    These less things hold my gaze!

Thomas Hardy (1840–1928)

A Green Cornfield

'And singing still dost soar and
　　Soaring ever singest.'

The earth was green, the sky was blue:
　　I saw and heard one sunny morn
A skylark hang between the two,
　　A singing speck above the corn;

A stage below, in gay accord,
　　White butterflies danced on the wing,
And still the singing skylark soared,
　　And silent sank and soared to sing.

The cornfield stretched a tender green
　　To right and left beside my walks;
I knew he had a nest unseen
　　Somewhere among the million stalks:

And as I paused to hear his song
　　While swift the sunny moments slid,
Perhaps his mate sat listening long,
　　And listened longer than I did.

Christina Rossetti (1830–1894)

To the Nightingale

Every night from even till morn,
Love's chorister amid the thorn
Is now so sweet a singer;
So sweet, as for her song I scorn
Apollo's voice and finger.

But nightingale, sith you delight
Ever to watch the starry night,
Tell all the stars of heaven,
Heaven never had a star so bright,
As now the earth is given.

Royal Astraea makes our day
Eternal with her beams, nor may
Gross darkness overcome her.
I now perceive why some do write,
No country hath so short a night,
As England hath in summer.

Sir John Davies (1569–1626)

The Soaking

The rain has come, and the earth must be very glad
Of its moisture, and the made roads all dust clad;
It lets a friendly veil down on the lucent dark,
And not of any bright ground thing shows any spark.

Tomorrow's grey morning will show cow-parsley,
Hung all with shining drops, and the river will be
Duller because of the all soddenness of things,
Till the skylark breaks his reluctance, hangs shaking, and sings.

Ivor Gurney (1890–1937)

The Sky Lark

The rolls and harrows lies at rest beside
The battered road; and spreading far and wide
Above the russet clods the corn is seen
Sprouting its spirey points of tender green
Where squats the hare to terrors wide awake
Like some brown clod the harrows failed to break
While neath the warm hedge boys stray far from home
To crop the early blossoms as they come
Where buttercups will make them eager run
Opening their golden caskets to the sun
To see who shall be first to pluck the prize
And from their hurry up the skylark flies
And oer her half formed nest with happy wings
Winnows the air – till in the cloud she sings
Then hangs a dust-spot in the sunny skies
And drops and drops till in her nest she lies
Which they unheeded past – neer dreaming then
That birds which flew so high – would drop agen
To nests upon the ground where any thing
May come at to destroy had they the wing
Like such a bird themselves would be too proud
And build on nothing but a passing cloud
As free from danger as the heavens are free
From pain and toil – there would they build and be
And sail about the world to scenes unheard
Of and unseen – O were they but a bird

So think they while they listen to its song,
And smile and fancy and so pass along
While its low nest moist with the dews of morn
Lye safely with the leveret in the corn

John Clare (1793–1864)

The Soote Season

The soote season, that bud and blome furth bringes,
With grene hath clad the hill and eke the vale:
The nightingale with fethers new she singes:
The turtle to her make hath tolde her tale:
Somer is come, for every spray nowe springes,
The hart hath hong his olde hed on the pale:
The buck in brake his winter cote he flinges:
The fishes flote with newe repaired scale:
The adder all her sloughe awaye she slinges:
The swift swalow pursueth the flyes smale:
The busy bee her honye now she minges:
Winter is worne that was the flowers bale:
And thus I see among these pleasant thinges
Eche care decayes, and yet my sorow springes.

Henry Howard, Earl of Surrey (c. 1517–1547)

Twilight Calm

Oh, pleasant eventide!
  Clouds on the western side
Grow grey and greyer hiding the warm sun:
The bees and birds, their happy labours done,
  Seek their close nests and bide.

Screened in the leafy wood
  The stock-doves sit and brood:
The very squirrel leaps from bough to bough
But lazily; pauses; and settles now
  Where once he stored his food.

One by one the flowers close,
  Lily and dewy rose
Shutting their tender petals from the moon:
The grasshoppers are still; but not so soon
  Are still the noisy crows.

The dormouse squats and eats
  Choice little dainty bits
Beneath the spreading roots of a broad lime;
Nibbling his fill he stops from time to time
  And listens where he sits.

From far the lowings come
  Of cattle driven home:
From farther still the wind brings fitfully
The vast continual murmur of the sea,
  Now loud, now almost dumb.

The gnats whirl in the air,
  The evening gnats; and there
The owl opes broad his eyes and wings to sail
For prey; the bat wakes; and the shell-less snail
  Comes forth, clammy and bare.

  Hark! that's the nightingale,
  Telling the selfsame tale
Her song told when this ancient earth was young:
So echoes answered when her song was sung
  In the first wooded vale.

  We call it love and pain
  The passion of her strain;
And yet we little understand or know:
Why should it not be rather joy that so
  Throbs in each throbbing vein?

  In separate herds the deer
  Lie; here the bucks, and here
The does, and by its mother sleeps the fawn:
Through all the hours of night until the dawn
  They sleep, forgetting fear.

  The hare sleeps where it lies,
  With wary half-closed eyes;
The cock has ceased to crow, the hen to cluck:
Only the fox is out, some heedless duck
  Or chicken to surprise.

Remote, each single star
    Comes out, till there they are
All shining brightly: how the dews fall damp!
While close at hand the glow-worm lights her lamp,
    Or twinkles from afar.

But evening now is done
    As much as if the sun
Day-giving had arisen in the East:
For night has come; and the great calm has ceased,
    The quiet sands have run.

Christina Rossetti (1830–1894)

A Barren Heath

FROM *THE LOVER'S JOURNEY*, LINES 34–45

First o'er a barren heath beside the coast
Orlando rode, and joy began to boast.

'This neat low gorse,' said he, 'with golden bloom,
Delights each sense, is beauty, is perfume;
And this gay ling, with all its purple flowers,
A man at leisure might admire for hours;
This green-fringed cup-moss has a scarlet tip,
That yields to nothing but my *Laura's* lip;
And then how fine this herbage! men may say
A heath is barren; nothing is so gay;
Barren or bare to call such charming scene,
Argues a mind possess'd by care and spleen.'

George Crabbe (1754–1832)

To a Skylark

VERSES 1–15

HAIL to thee, blithe Spirit!
  Bird thou never wert,
That from Heaven, or near it,
  Pourest thy full heart
In profuse strains of unpremeditated art.

Higher still and higher
  From the earth thou springest
Like a cloud of fire;
  The blue deep thou wingest,
And singing still dost soar, and soaring ever singest.

In the golden lightning
  Of the sunken sun,
O'er which clouds are bright'ning,
  Thou dost float and run;
Like an unbodied joy whose race is just begun.

The pale purple even
  Melts around thy flight;
Like a star of heaven
  In the broad daylight
Thou art unseen, but yet I hear thy shrill delight,

Keen as are the arrows
  Of that silver sphere,
Whose intense lamp narrows
  In the white dawn clear
Until we hardly see – we feel that it is there.

All the earth and air
    With thy voice is loud,
As, when night is bare,
    From one lonely cloud
The moon rains out her beams, and Heaven is overflowed.

What thou art we know not;
    What is most like thee?
From rainbow clouds there flow not
    Drops so bright to see
As from thy presence showers a rain of melody.

Like a Poet hidden
    In the light of thought,
Singing hymns unbidden,
    Till the world is wrought
To sympathy with hopes and fears it heeded not:

Like a high-born maiden
    In a palace-tower,
Soothing her love-laden
    Soul in secret hour
With music sweet as love, which overflows her bower:

Like a glow-worm golden
    In a dell of dew,
Scattering unbeholden
    Its aëreal hue
Among the flowers and grass, which screen it from the view!

Like a rose embowered
    In its own green leaves,
By warm winds deflowered,
    Till the scent it gives
Makes faint with too much sweet those heavy-wingèd thieves:

Sound of vernal showers
    On the twinkling grass,
Rain-awakened flowers,
    All that ever was
Joyous, and clear, and fresh, thy music doth surpass:

Teach us, Sprite or Bird,
    What sweet thoughts are thine:
I have never heard
    Praise of love or wine
That painted forth a flood of rapture so divine.

Chorus Hymeneal,
    Or triumphal chant,
Matched with thine would be all
    But an empty vaunt,
A thing wherein we feel there is some hidden want.

What objects are the fountains
    Of thy happy strain?
What fields, or waves, or mountains?
    What shapes of sky or plain?
What love of thine own kind? what ignorance of pain?

Percy Bysshe Shelley (1792–1822)

Botanical Nomenclature

Down East people, not being botanists,
call it 'that pink-and-blue flower
you find along the shore.' Wildflower
guides, their minds elsewhere, mumble
'sea lungwort or oysterleaf' as a label
for these recumbent roundels, foliage
blued to a driftwood patina
growing outward, sometimes to the
size of a cathedral window,
stemrib grisaille edge-tasseled
with opening goblets, with bugles
in miniature, mauve through cerulean,
toggled in a seaweed scree,
these tuffets of skyweed
neighbored by a climbing tideline,
by the holdfasts, the gargantuan lariats
of kelp, a landfall of seaweed:

Mertensia, the learned Latin
handle,proving the uses of taxonomy,
shifts everything abruptly inland,
childhoodward, to what we called then
(though not properly) bluebells:
spring-bottomland glades standing upright,
their lake-evoking sky color
a trapdoor, a window letting in distances
all the way to the ocean –
reaching out, *nolens volens*,
as one day everything breathing
will reach out, with just such

bells on its fingers, to touch
without yet quite having seen
the unlikelihood, the ramifying
happenstance, the mirroring
marryings of all likeness.

Amy Clampitt (1920–1994)

In the Forest

Out of the mid-wood's twilight
    Into the meadow's dawn,
Ivory-limbed and brown-eyed,
    Flashes my Faun!

He skips through the copses singing,
    And his shadow dances along,
And I know not which I should follow,
    Shadow or song!

O Hunter, snare me his shadow!
    O Nightingale, catch me his strain!
Else moonstruck with music and madness
    I track him in vain.

Oscar Wilde (1854–1900)

Leopards at Knole

Leopards on the gable-ends,
Leopards on the painted stair,
Stiff the blazoned shield they bear,
Or and gules, a bend of vair,
Leopards on the gable-ends,
    Leopards everywhere.

Guard and vigil in the night
While the ancient house is sleeping
They three hundred years are keeping,
Nightly from their stations leaping,
Shadows black in moonlight bright,
    Roof to gable creeping.

Rigid when the day returns,
Up aloft in sun or rain
Leopards at their posts again
Watch the shifting pageant's train;
And their jewelled colour burns
    In the window-pane.

Often on the painted stair,
As I passed abstractedly,
Velvet footsteps, two and three,
Padded gravely after me.
– There was nothing, nothing there,
    Nothing there to see.

Vita Sackville-West (1892–1962)

Love in a Mist

Light love in a mist, by the midsummer moon misguided,
Scarce seen in the twilight garden if gloom insist,
Seems vainly to seek for a star whose gleam has derided
　　Light love in a mist.

All day in the sun, when the breezes do all they list,
His soft blue raiment of cloudlike blossom abided
Unrent and unwithered of winds and of rays that kissed.

Blithe-hearted or sad, as the cloud or the sun subsided,
Love smiled in the flower with a meaning whereof none wist
Save two that beheld, as a gleam that before them glided,
　　Light love in a mist.

Algernon Charles Swinburne (1837–1909)

The Kingfisher

It was the Rainbow gave thee birth,
    And left thee all her lovely hues;
And, as her mother's name was Tears,
    So runs it in my blood to choose
For haunts the lonely pools, and keep
In company with the trees that weep.

Go you, with such glorious hues,
    Live with proud Peacocks in green parks;
On lawns as smooth as shining glass,
    Let every feather show its marks;
Get thee on boughs and clap thy wings
Before the windows of proud kings.

Nay, lovely Bird, thou art not vain;
    Thou hast no proud ambitious mind;
I also love a quiet place
    That's green, away from all mankind;
A lonely pool, and let a tree
Sigh with her bosom over me.

W. H. Davies (1871–1940)

The Sixt Nimphall

LINES 1–20

Cleere had the day bin from the dawne,
All chequered was the Skye,
Thin Clouds like Scarfs of Cobweb Lawne
Vayld Heaven's most glorious eye.
The Winde had no more strength than this,
That leisurely it blew,
To make one leafe the next to kisse,
That closely by it grew.
The Rills that on the Pebbles playd,
Might now be heard at will;
This world they onely Musick made,
Else everything was still.
The Flowers like brave embraudred Girles,
Lookt as they much desired,
To see whose head with orient Pearles
Most curiously was tyred;
And to it selfe the subtle Ayre,
Such soverainty assumes,
That it receiv'd too large a share
From natures rich perfumes.

Michael Drayton (1563–1631)

My Heart Leaps Up When I Behold

WRITTEN AT TOWN-END, GRASMERE

My heart leaps up when I behold
    A rainbow in the sky:
So it was when my life began;
So it is now I am a man;
So be it when I shall grow old,
    Or let me die!
The Child is father of the Man;
And I could wish my days to be
Bound each to each by natural piety.

William Wordsworth (1770–1850)

Ariel's Song

FROM *THE TEMPEST*, ACT V SCENE I

Where the bee sucks, there suck I:
In a cowslip's bell I lie;
There I couch when owls do cry.
On the bat's back I do fly
After summer merrily.
Merrily, merrily shall I live now
Under the blossom that hangs on the bough.

William Shakespeare (1564–1616)

Dover Beach

The sea is calm to-night.
The tide is full, the moon lies fair
Upon the straits; – on the French coast the light
Gleams and is gone; the cliffs of England stand,
Glimmering and vast, out in the tranquil bay.
Come to the window, sweet is the night air!
Only, from the ling line of spray
Where the sea meets the moon-blanch'd land,
Listen! you hear the grating roar
Of pebbles which the waves draw back, and fling,
At their return, up the high strand,
Begin, and cease, and then again begin,
With tremulous cadence slow, and bring
The eternal note of sadness in.

Sophocles long ago
Heard it on the Ægæan, and it brought
Into his mind the turbid ebb and flow
Of human misery; we
Find also in the sound a thought,
Hearing it by this distant northern sea.

The Sea of Faith
Was once, at the full, and round earth's shore
Lay like the folds of a bright girdle furl'd.
But now I only hear
Its melancholy, long, withdrawing roar,
Retreating, to the breath
Of the night-wind, down the vast edges drear
And naked shingles of this world.

Ah, love, let us be true
To one another! for the world, which seems
To lie before us like a land of dreams,
So various, so beautiful, so new,
Hath really neither joy, nor love, nor light,
Nor certitude, nor peace, nor help for pain;
And we are here as on a darkling plain
Swept with confused alarms of struggle and flight,
Where ignorant armies clash by night.

Matthew Arnold (1822–1888)

The Kingfisher

The Kingfisher perches. He studies.

Escaped from the jeweller's opium
X-rays the river's toppling
Tangle of glooms.

Now he's vanished – into vibrations.
A sudden electric wire, jarred rigid,
Snaps – with a blue flare.

He has left his needle buried in your ear.

Oafish oaks, kneeling, bend over
Dragging with their reflections
For the sunken stones. The Kingfisher
Erupts through the mirror, beak full of ingots,

And is away – cutting the one straight line
Of the raggle-taggle tumbledown river
With a diamond –

Leaves a rainbow splinter sticking in your eye.

Through him, God, whizzing in the sun,
Glimpses the angler.

Through him, God
Marries a pit
Of fishy mire.
          And look! He's
– gone again.
          Spark, sapphire, refracted
From beyond water
Shivering the spine of the river.

Ted Hughes (1930–1998)

High Summer

I never wholly feel that summer is high,
However green the trees, or loud the birds,
However movelessly eye winking herds,
Stand in field ponds, or under large trees lie, –
Till I do climb all cultured pastures by,
That hedged by hedgerows studiously fretted trim,
Smile like a lady's face with lace laced prim,
And on some moor or hill that seeks the sky
Lonely and nakedly, – utterly lie down,
And feel the sunshine throbbing on body and limb,
My drowsy brain in pleasant drunkenness swim,
Each rising thought sink back, and dreamily drown,
Smiles creep o'er my face, and smother my lips, and cloy,
Each muscle sink to itself, and separately enjoy.

Ebenezer Jones (1820–1860)

The Orchard

Almond, apple, and peach,
Walnut, cherry, plum,
Ash, chestnut, and beech,
And lime and sycamore
We have planted for days to come;

No stony monument
But growing, changing things,
Leaf, fruit, and honied scent,
Bloom that the bees explore,
Sprays where the bird sings.

In other Junes than ours
When the boughs spread and rise
Tall into leafy towers
To grace and guard this small
Corner of paradise;

When petals red and white
Resign to warming air,
Without speech or sight
From our hands they will fall
On happy voices there.

Laurence Binyon (1869–1943)

The Unknown Bird

Three lovely notes he whistled, too soft to be heard
If others sang; but others never sang
In the great beech-wood all that May and June.
No one saw him: I alone could hear him
Though many listened. Was it but four years
Ago? or five? He never came again.

Oftenest when I heard him I was alone,
Nor could I ever make another hear.
La-la-la! he called, seeming far-off –
As if a cock crowed past the edge of the world,
As if the bird or I were in a dream.
Yet that he travelled through the trees and sometimes
Neared me, was plain, though somehow distant still
He sounded. All the proof is – I told men
What I had heard.

       I never knew a voice,
Man, beast, or bird, better than this. I told
The naturalists; but neither had they heard
Anything like the notes that did so haunt me,
I had them clear by heart and have them still.
Four years, or five, have made no difference. Then
As now that La-la-la! was bodiless sweet:
Sad more than joyful it was, if I must say
That it was one or other, but if sad
'Twas sad only with joy too, too far off
For me to taste it. But I cannot tell
If truly never anything but fair
The days were when he sang, as now they seem.
This surely I know, that I who listened then,

Happy sometimes, sometimes suffering
A heavy body and a heavy heart,
Now straightway, if I think of it, become
Light as that bird wandering beyond my shore.

Edward Thomas (1878–1917)

Yellow Iris

It's early morning
and a woman
from a previous
world is wading
up the stream.

Very stately and
sturdy with double-
jointed elbows she's
still in her
grave clothes,
her crinkled three-ply
surcoat made of
cloth of June.

She has one
gold-webbed glove,
one withered hand.

She's resting, considering
her next pose,
behind the blades
of slatted blinds.

Her name is
Iris, the Rainbow,
the messenger, the
water's secretary, the
only word she
speaks is 'yellow'.

Lost ghost Queen
of the Unbetween
it's lovely listening
to the burp
of mud as
she sinks her
feet right in.

Alice Oswald (1966–)

The Windhover

TO CHRIST OUR LORD

I caught this morning morning's minion, king-
    dom of daylight's dauphin, dapple-dawn-drawn Falcon, in his riding
    Of the rolling level underneath him steady air, and striding
High there, how he rung upon the rein of a wimpling wing
In his ecstasy! then off, off forth on swing,
    As a skate's heel sweeps smooth on a bow-bend: the hurl and gliding
    Rebuffed the big wind. My heart in hiding
Stirred for a bird, – the achieve of, the mastery of the thing!

Brute beauty and valour and act, oh, air, pride, plume, here
    Buckle! AND the fire that breaks from thee then, a billion
Times told lovelier, more dangerous, O my chevalier!

    No wonder of it: shéer plód makes plough down sillion
Shine, and blue-bleak embers, ah my dear,
    Fall, gall themselves, and gash gold-vermilion.

Gerard Manley Hopkins (1844–1889)

Cape Ann

O quick quick quick, quick hear the song-sparrow,
Swamp-sparrow, fox-sparrow, vesper-sparrow
At dawn and dusk. Follow the dance
Of the goldfinch at noon. Leave to chance
The Blackburnian warbler, the shy one. Hail
With shrill whistle the note of the quail, the bob-white
Dodging by bay-bush. Follow the feet
Of the walker, the water-thrush. Follow the flight
Of the dancing arrow, the purple martin. Greet
In silence the bullbat. All are delectable. Sweet sweet sweet
But resign this land at the end, resign it
To its true owner, the tough one, the sea-gull.

The palaver is finished.

T. S. Eliot (1888–1965)

The Mower to the Glo-Worms

I

Ye living Lamps, by whose dear light
The Nightingale does sit so late,
And studying all the Summer-night,
Her matchless Songs does meditate;

II

Ye Country Comets, that portend
No War, nor Prince's funeral,
Shining unto no higher end
Than to presage the Grasses fall;

III

Ye Glo-worms, whose officious Flame
To wandring Mowers shows the way.
That in the Night have lost their aim,
And after foolish Fires do stray;

IV

Your courteous Lights in vain you waste,
Since *Juliana* here is come,
For She my Mind hath so displac'd
That I shall never find my home.

Andrew Marvell (1621–1678)

English Wild Flowers

Forget the Latin names; the English ones
Are gracious and specific. Hedge-rows are
Quickening fast with vetch and cow-parsley.
And fast along the lawn the daisies rise
For chains or the murdering lawn-mower.

Look everywhere, there is all botany
Laid between rising corn,
Infesting hay-fields. Look, the buttercup
Stares at the sun and seems to take a share
Of wealthy light. It glows beneath our chins.

Slim shepherd's purse is lost in dandelions,
Scabious will show a little later. See,
The dog-rose in the hedge. It dies at once
When you pluck it. Forget-me-nots disclose
Points of pure blue, the sovereign blue of the sky.
And then there are the herbs.

Counting this floral beauty I grow warm
With patriotism. These are my own flowers,
Springing to pleasant life in my own nation.
The times are dark but never too dark for
An Eden Summer, this flower-rich creation.

Elizabeth Jennings (1926–2001)

The Bee

The Pedigree of Honey
Does not concern the Bee;
A Clover, any time, to him
Is Aristocracy.

Emily Dickinson (1830–1886)

Verses Written in a Garden

See how the pair of billing doves
With open murmurs own their loves;
And, heedless of censorious eyes,
Pursue their unpolluted joys:
No fears of future want molest
The downy quiet of their nest:
No interest joined the happy pair,
Securely blest in Nature's care,
While her dear dictates they pursue:
For constancy is nature too.

   Can all the doctrine of our schools,
Our moral maxims, our religious rules,
Can learning, to our lives ensure
Virtue so bright, or bliss so pure?
The great Creator's happy hand
Virtue and pleasure ever blends:
In vain the Church and Court have tried
Th' united essence to divide:
Alike they find their wild mistake,
The pedant priest, and giddy rake.

Lady Mary Wortley Montagu (1689–1762)

JULY

The Larkspurs Stood Like Sentinels

Summer Vacation

FROM *THE PRELUDE*, BOOK FOURTH, LINES 1–11

Bright was the summer's noon when quickening steps
Followed each other till a dreary moor
Was crossed, a bare ridge clomb, upon whose top
Standing alone, as from a rampart's edge,
I overlooked the bed of Windermere,
Like a vast river, stretching in the sun.
With exultation, at my feet I saw
Lake, islands, promontories, gleaming bays,
A universe of Nature's fairest forms
Proudly revealed with instantaneous burst,
Magnificent, and beautiful, and gay.

William Wordsworth (1770–1850)

To Mrs Boteler, A Description of her Garden

VERSES 1–9

How charming is this little spot
Disposed with art and taste.
A thousand beauties intermixed
Prepare the eyes a feast.

The lovely limes in ample rows
With woodbines climbing round,
A shining gravel walk inclose
Where not a weed is found.

The crocus, primrose, daffodil,
And cowslip sweet I sing,
And fragrant purple violet –
All harbingers of spring;

The musky blushing lovely pink,
Jonquil with rich perfume,
Tulips that vie with Iris' bow,
And balsam's annual bloom;

The immortal pea, fair 'emone,
And beamy marigold,
And polyanthus (lovely tribe!)
Their various blooms unfold.

The gardener's pride, ranunculus,
Bell-flowered ethereal blue,
The rose campion, and golden lupe,
And wonder of Peru;

The amaranths, as poets sing,
That Juno deigned to wear,
That in Hesperian gardens spring,
Bloom fair and fragrant here.

The lily fair as new-fallen snow;
All these the borders grace,
And myrtles, roses, jessamines
With fragrance fill the place.

A group of dwarfish apple trees
Appear, a fairy scene,
Laden with fruit, such Paris gave
To Venus, beauty's queen.

Mary Chandler (1687–1745)

Flying Crooked

The butterfly, the cabbage-white,
(His honest idiocy of flight)
Will never now, it is too late,
Master the art of flying straight,
Yet has – who knows so well as I? –
A just sense of how not to fly:
He lurches here and here by guess
And God and hope and hopelessness.
Even the acrobatic swift
Has not his flying-crooked gift.

Robert Graves (1895–1985)

Sonnet: To the Poppy

While summer roses all their glory yield
    To crown the votary of love and joy,
    Misfortune's victim hails, with many a sigh,
    Thee, scarlet Poppy of the pathless field,
Gaudy, yet wild and lone; no leaf to shield
    Thy flaccid vest that, as the gale blows high,
    Flaps, and alternate folds around thy head.
    So stands in the long grass a love-crazed maid,
Smiling aghast; while stream to every wind
    Her garish ribbons, smeared with dust and rain;
    But brain-sick visions cheat her totured mind,
And bring false peace. Thus, lulling grief and pain,
    Kind dreams oblivious from thy juice proceed,
    Thou flimsy, showy, melancholy weed.

Anna Seward (1742–1809)

Otter In and Out

Collision of opposites which pulls the river
plucks the otter through an aperture
and lays and breeds the river, high and low,
through Dipper Mill in her absorbing beauty;

and brings us running from the field
and throws and cleaves us into shadows
arm in arm and apart upon the water;
and flexes the otter in and out of the water.

The whole river transforms upon an otter.
Now and gone, sometimes we see him
swimming above the fish – half-of-the-air,
half-of-the-darkness – when he dives,

a duck-flip into darkness, creep
close to the edge and closer. There are times
when water's attentiveness
is tight enough to walk on

and we came so strangely
out of the darkness to this world
of watersounds colliding slowly,
out and in and disappear in darkness ...

Alice Oswald (1966–)

Evening Star

'Twas noontide of summer,
    And mid-time of night;
And stars, in their orbits,
    Shone pale, thro' the light
Of the brighter, cold moon,
    'Mid planets her slaves,
Herself in the Heavens,
    Her beam on the waves.
    I gaz'd awhile
    On her cold smile;
Too cold – too cold for me –
    There pass'd, as a shroud,
    A fleecy cloud,
And I turn'd away to thee,
    Proud Evening Star,
    In thy glory afar,
And dearer thy beam shall be;
    For joy to my heart
    Is the proud part
Thou bearest in Heav'n at night,
    And more I admire
    Thy distant fire,
Than that colder, lowly light.

Edgar Allan Poe (1809–1849)

The Garden

VERSES I AND II

I
How vainly men themselves amaze
To win the Palm, the Oke or Bayes,
And their uncessant Labours see
Crown'd from some single Herb or Tree,
Whose short and narrow verged Shade
Does prudently their Toyles upbraid,
While all Flow'rs and all Trees do close
To weave the Garlands of repose.

II
Fair quiet, have I found thee here,
And Innocence, thy Sister dear!
Mistaken long, I sought you then
In busie Companies of Men.
Your sacred Plants, if here below,
Only among the Plants will grow.
Society is all but rude,
To this delicious Solitude.

Andrew Marvell (1621–1678)

The Hawk

'Call down the hawk from the air;
Let him be hooded or caged
Till the yellow eye has grown mild,
For larder and spit are bare,
The old cook enraged,
The scullion gone wild.'

'I will not be clapped in a hood,
Nor a cage, nor alight upon wrist,
Now I have learnt to be proud
Hovering over the wood
In the broken mist
Or tumbling cloud.'

'What tumbling cloud did you cleave,
Yellow-eyed hawk of the mind,
Last evening? that I, who had sat
Dumbfounded before a knave,
Should give to my friend
A pretence of wit.'

W. B. Yeats (1865–1939)

Evening

QUATRAINS I–IV

The Day's grown old, the fainting Sun
Has but a little way to run,
And yet his Steeds, with all his skill,
Scarce lug the Chariot down the Hill.

With Labour spent, and Thirst opprest,
Whilst they strain hard to gain the West,
From Fetlocks hot drops melted light,
Which turns to Meteors in the Night.

The shadows now so long do grow
That Brambles like tall Cedars show,
Mole-hills seem Mountains, and the Ant
Appears a monstrous Elephant.

A very little little Flock
Shades thrice the ground that it would stock;
Whilst the small Stripling following them,
Appears a mighty *Polypheme*.

Charles Cotton (1630–1687)

To the Bramble Flower

Thy fruit full well the school-boy knows,
     Wild bramble of the brake!
So, put thou forth thy small white rose;
     I love it for his sake.
Though woodbines flaunt and roses glow
     O'er all the fragrant bowers,
Thou need'st not be ashamed to show
     Thy satin-threaded flowers;
For dull the eye, the heart is dull,
     That cannot feel how fair,
Amid all beauty beautiful,
     Thy tender blossoms are!
How delicate thy gauzy frill!
     How rich thy branchy stem!
How soft thy voice, when woods are still,
     And thou sing'st hymns to them;
While silent showers are falling slow,
     And, 'mid the general hush,
A sweet air lifts the little bough,
     Lone whispering through the bush!
The primrose to the grave is gone;
     The hawthorn flower is dead;
The violet by the moss'd grey stone
     Hath laid her weary head;
But thou, wild bramble! back dost bring,
     In all thy beauteous power,
The fresh green days of life's fair spring,
     And boyhood's blossomy hour.

Scorn'd bramble of the brake! once more
    Thou bid'st me be a boy,
To gad with thee the woodlands o'er,
    In freedom and in joy.

Ebenezer Elliott (1781–1849)

Like Rain it Soundeth

Like Rain it soundeth till it curved
And then I knew 'twas Wind –
It walked as wet as any Wave
But swept as dry as sand –
When it had pushed itself away
To some remotest Plain
A coming of the Hosts was heard
And that indeed was Rain –
It filled the Wells, it pleased the Pools
It warbled in the Road –
It pulled the spigot from the Hills
And let the Floods abroad –
It loosened acres, lifted seas
The sites of Centres stirred
Then like Elijah rode away
Upon a Wheel of Cloud.

Emily Dickinson (1830–1886)

To the Daisy

Bright Flower! whose home is everywhere,
Bold in maternal Nature's care,
And all the long year through the heir
    Of joy or sorrow;
Methinks that there abides in thee
Some concord with humanity,
Given to no other flower I see
    The forest thorough!

Is it that Man is soon deprest?
A thoughtless Thing! who, once unblest,
Does little on his memory rest,
    Or on his reason,
And Thou would'st teach him how to find
A shelter under every wind,
A hope for times that are unkind
    And every season?

Thou wander'st the wide world about,
Uncheck'd by pride or scrupulous doubt,
With friend to greet thee, or without,
    Yet pleased and willing;
Meek, yielding to the occasion's call,
And all things suffering from all,
Thy function apostolical
    In peace fulfilling.

William Wordsworth (1770–1850)

The Little Crocodile

How doth the little crocodile
　　Improve his shining tail
And pour the waters of the Nile
　　On every shining scale!

How cheerfully he seems to grin,
　　How neatly spreads his claws,
And welcomes little fishes in
　　With gently smiling jaws!

Lewis Carroll (1832–1898)

Jenny Wren

Her sight is short, she comes quite near;
A foot to me's a mile to her;
And she is known as Jenny Wren,
The smallest bird in England. When
I heard that little bird at first,
Methought her frame would surely burst
With earnest song. Oft had I seen
Her running under leaves so green,
Or in the grass when fresh and wet,
As though her wings she would forget.
And, seeing this, I said to her –
'My pretty runner, you prefer
To be a thing to run unheard
Through leaves and grass, and not a bird!'
'Twas then she burst, to prove me wrong,
Into a sudden storm of song;
So very loud and earnest, I
Feared she would break her heart and die.
'Nay, nay,' I laughed, 'be you no thing
To run unheard, sweet scold, but sing!
O I could hear your voice near me,
Above the din in that oak tree,
When almost all the twigs on top
Had starlings chattering without stop.'

W. H. Davies (1871–1940)

St Swithun's Day

St Swithun's day if thou dost rain
For forty-days it will remain
St Swithun's day if thou be fair
For forty days 'twill rain nae mare

Anon

Ducks' Ditty

FROM *WIND IN THE WILLOWS*

All along the backwater,
Through the rushes tall,
Ducks are a-dabbling.
Up tails all!

Ducks' tails, drakes' tails,
Yellow feet a-quiver,
Yellow bills out of sight
Busy in the river!

Slushy green undergrowth
Where the roach swim –
Here we keep our larder,
Cool and full and dim.

Everyone for what he likes!
We like to be
Head down, tails up,
Dabbling free!

High in the blue above
Swifts whirl and call –
We are down a-dabbling
Up tails all!

Kenneth Grahame (1859–1932)

The Way Through the Woods

They shut the road through the woods
Seventy years ago.
Weather and rain have undone it again,
And now you would never know
There was once a road through the woods
Before they planted the trees.
It is underneath the coppice and heath
And the thin anemones.
Only the keeper sees
That, where the ring-dove broods,
And the badgers roll at ease,
There was once a road through the woods.

Yet, if you enter the woods
Of a summer evening late,
When the night-air cools on the trout-ringed pools
Where the otter whistles his mate,
(They fear not men in the woods,
Because they see so few.)
You will hear the beat of a horse's feet,
And the swish of a skirt in the dew,
Steadily cantering through
The misty solitudes,
As though they perfectly knew
The old lost road through the woods ...
But there is no road through the woods.

Rudyard Kipling (1865–1936)

Dogs and Weather

I'd like a different dog
　　For every kind of weather –
A narrow greyhound for a fog,
　　A wolfhound strange and white,
With a tail like a silver feather
　　To run with in the night,
　　When snow is still, and winter stars are bright.

In the fall I'd like to see
　　In answer to my whistle,
A golden spaniel look at me.
　　But best of all for rain
A terrier, hairy as a thistle,
　　To trot with fine disdain
　　Beside me down the soaked, sweet-smelling lane.

Winifred Welles (1893–1939)

Winged Words

As darting swallows skim across a pool,
    Whose tranquil depths reflect a tranquil sky,
So, o'er the depths of silence, dark and cool,
        Our winged words dart playfully,
            And seldom break
        The quiet surface of the lake,
            As they flit by.

Mary Coleridge (1861–1907)

Leaves Compared with Flowers

A tree's leaves may be ever so good,
So may its bar, so may its wood;
But unless you put the right thing to its root
It never will show much flower or fruit.

But I may be one who does not care
Ever to have tree bloom or bear.
Leaves for smooth and bark for rough,
Leaves and bark may be tree enough.

Some giant trees have bloom so small
They might as well have none at all.
Late in life I have come on fern.
Now lichens are due to have their turn.

I bade men tell me which in brief,
Which is fairer, flower or leaf.
They did not have the wit to say,
Leaves by night and flowers by day.

Leaves and bar, leaves and bark,
To lean against and hear in the dark.
Petals I may have once pursued.
Leaves are all my darker mood.

Robert Frost (1874–1963)

A Lake

A lake
Is a river curled and asleep like a snake.

Thomas Lovell Beddoes (1803–1849)

James Thomson: The Shelving Brink

FROM *SUMMER, THE SEASONS*

Smooth to the shelving brink a copious flood
Rolls fair and placid: where collected all,
In one impetuous torrent, down the steep
It thundering shoots, and shakes the country round.
At first, an azure sheet, it rushes broad;
Then whitening by degrees, as prone it falls,
And from the loud-resounding rocks below
Dash'd in a cloud of foam, it sends aloft
A hoary mist, and forms a ceaseless shower.
Nor can the tortured wave here find repose:
But, raging still amid the shaggy rocks,
Now flashes o'er the scatter'd fragments, now
Aslant the hollow channel rapid darts;
And falling fast from gradual slope to slope,
With wild infracted course, and lessen'd roar,
It gains a safer bed, and steals, at last,
Along the mazes of the quiet vale.

James Thomson (1700–1748)

The Glory of the Garden

Our England is a garden that is full of stately views,
Of borders, beds and shrubberies and lawns and avenues,
With statues on the terraces and peacocks strutting by;
But the Glory of the Garden lies in more than meets the eye.

For where the old thick laurels grow, along the thin red wall,
You find the tool- and potting-sheds which are the heart of all;
The cold-frames and the hot-houses, the dungpits and the tanks,
The rollers, carts and drain-pipes, with the barrows and the planks.

And there you'll see the gardeners, the men and 'prentice boys
Told off to do as they are bid and do it without noise;
For, except when seeds are planted and we shout to scare the birds,
The Glory of the Garden it abideth not in words.

And some can pot begonias and some can bud a rose,
And some are hardly fit to trust with anything that grows;
But they can roll and trim the lawns and sift the sand and loam,
For the Glory of the Garden occupieth all who come.

Our England is a garden, and such gardens are not made
By singing: – 'Oh, how beautiful!' and sitting in the shade,
While better men than we go out and start their working lives
At grubbing weeds from gravel-paths with broken dinner-knives.

There's not a pair of legs so thin, there's not a head so thick,
There's not a hand so weak and white, nor yet a heart so sick,
But it can find some needful job that's crying to be done,
For the Glory of the Garden glorifieth everyone.

Then seek your job with thankfulness and work till further orders,
If it's only netting strawberries or killing slugs in borders;
And when your back stops aching and your hands begin to harden,
You will find yourself a partner in the Glory of the Garden.

Oh, Adam was a gardener, and God who made him sees
That half a proper gardener's work is done upon his knees,
So when your work is finished, you can wash your hands and pray
For the Glory of the Garden, that it may not pass away!
And the Glory of the Garden it shall never pass away!

Rudyard Kipling (1865–1936)

On the Grasshopper and the Cricket

The poetry of earth is never dead:
    When all the birds are faint with the hot sun,
    And hide in cooling trees, a voice will run
From hedge to hedge about the new-mown mead;
That is the Grasshopper's – he takes the lead
    In summer luxury, – he has never done
    With his delights; for when tired out with fun
He rests at ease beneath some pleasant weed.
The poetry of earth is ceasing never:
    On a lone winter evening, when the frost
        Has wrought a silence, from the stove there shrills
The Cricket's song, in warmth increasing ever,
    And seems to one in drowsiness half lost,
        The Grasshopper's among some grassy hills.

John Keats (1795–1821)

Flowers

What favourite flowers are mine, I cannot say –
My fancy changes with the summer's day.
Sometimes I think, agreeing with the Bees,
That my best flowers are those tall apple trees,
Who give a Bee his cyder while in bloom,
And keep me waiting till their apples come.
Sometimes I think the Columbine has won,
Who hangs her head and never looks the Sun
Straight in the face. And now the Golden Rod
Beckons me over with a graceful nod;
Shaped like a sheaf of corn, her ruddy skin
Drinks the Sun dry, and leaves his splendour thin.
Sometimes I think the Rose must have her place –
And then the Lily shakes her golden dice
Deep in a silver cup, to win or lose.
So I go on, from Columbine to Rose,
From Marigold to Flock, from Flock to Thrift –
Till nothing but my garden stones are left.
But when I see the dimples in her face,
All filled with tender moss in every place –
Ah, then I think, when all is said and done,
My favourite flower must be a Mossy Stone!

W. H. Davies (1871–1940)

When First the Eye this Forrest Sees

FROM *UPON APPLETON HOUSE TO MY LORD FAIRFAX*, LXIII

When first the Eye this Forest sees
It seems indeed as *Wood* not *Trees*:
As if their Neighbourhood so old
To one great Trunk them all did mold.
There the huge Bulk takes place, as ment
To thrust up a *Fifth Element*;
And stretched still so closely wedg'd
As if the Night within were hedg'd.

Andrew Marvell (1621–1678)

The Naturalist's Summer-Evening Walk

TO THOMAS PENNANT, ESQ.

When day declining sheds a milder gleam,
What time the may-fly haunts the pool or stream;
When the still owl skims round the grassy mead,
What time the timorous hare limps forth to feed;
Then be the time to steal adown the vale,
And listen to the vagrant cuckoo's tale;
To hear the clamorous curlew call his mate,
Or the soft quail his tender pain relate;
To see the swallow sweep the dark'ning plain
Belated, to support her infant train;
To mark the swift in rapid giddy ring
Dash round the steeple, unsubdued of wing:
Amusive birds! – say where your hid retreat
When the frost rages and the tempests beat;
Whence your return, by such nice instinct led,
When spring, soft season, lifts her bloomy head?
Such baffled searches mock man's prying pride,
The God of Nature is your secret guide!
　　While deep'ning shades obscure the face of day,
To yonder bench leaf-sheltered let us stray,
Till blended objects fail the swimming sight,
And all the fading landscape sinks in night;
To hear the drowsy dor come brushing by
With buzzing wing, or the shrill cricket cry;
To see the feeding bat glance through the wood;
To catch the distant falling of the flood;
While o'er the cliff th'awakened churn-owl hung
Through the still gloom protracts his chattering song;
While high in air, and poised upon his wings,
Unseen, the soft, enamoured woodlark sings:

These, Nature's works, the curious mind employ,
Inspire a soothing melancholy joy:
As fancy warms, a pleasing kind of pain
Steals o'er the cheek, and thrills the creeping vein!
    Each rural sight, each sound, each smell, combine;
The tinkling sheep-bell, or the breath of kine;
The new-mown hay that scents the swelling breeze,
Or cottage-chimney smoking through the trees.
    The chilling night-dews fall: away, retire;
For see, the glow-worm lights her amorous fire!
Thus, ere night's veil had half obscured the sky,
Th'impatient damsel hung her lamp on high:
True to the signal, by love's meteor led,
Leander hastened to his Hero's bed.

Gilbert White (1720–1793)

Sweet Suffolke Owle

Sweet, Suffolke Owle, so trimly dight,
With feathers, like a Lady bright,
Thou sing'st alone, sitting, by night,
Te whit, te whoo!
Thy note that forth so freely roules,
With shrill command the Mouse controules,
And sings a dirge for dying soules,
Te whit, te whoo!

Thomas Vautor (fl. c.1590–1619)

The Bullfinches

Brother Bulleys, let us sing
From the dawn till evening! –
For we know not that we go not
When to-day's pale pinions fold
Unto those who sang of old.

When I flew to Blackmoor Vale,
Whence the green-gowned faeries hail,
Roosting near them I could hear them
Speak of queenly Nature's ways,
Means, and moods, – well known to fays.

All we creatures, nigh and far
(Said they there), the Mother's are:
Yet she never shows endeavour
To protect from warrings wild
Bird or beast she calls her child.

Busy in her handsome house
Known as Space, she falls a-drowse;
Yet, in seeming, works on dreaming,
While beneath her groping hands
Fiends make havoc in her bands.

How her hussif'ry succeeds
She unknows or she unheeds,
All things making for Death's taking!
– So the green-gowned faeries say
Living over Blackmoor way.

Come then, brethren, let us sing,
From the dawn till evening! –
For we know not that we go not
    When the day's pale pinions fold
    Where those be that sang of old.

Thomas Hardy (1840–1928)

Song

The summer down the garden walks
    Swept in her garments bright;
She touched the pale still lily stalks
    And crowned them with delight;
She breathed upon the rose's head
    And filled its heart with fire,
And with a golden carpet spread
    The path of my desire.

The larkspurs stood like sentinels
    To greet her as she came,
Soft rang the Canterbury bells
    The music of her name.
She passed across the happy land
    Where all dear dreams flower free;
She took my true love by the hand
    And led her out to me.

E. Nesbit (1854–1924)

Brown and Furry

Brown and furry
Caterpillar in a hurry,
Take your walk
To the shady leaf, or stalk,
Or what not,
Which may be the chosen spot.
No toad spy you,
Hovering bird of prey pass by you;
Spin and die,
To live again a butterfly.

Christina Rossetti (1830–1894)

AUGUST

The Glimmering Landscape

Elegy Written in a Country Churchyard

VERSES 1–9

The curfew tolls the knell of parting day,
The lowing herd wind slowly o'er the lea,
The plowman homeward plods his weary way,
And leaves the world to darkness and to me.

Now fades the glimmering landscape on the sight,
And all the air a solemn stillness holds,
Save where the beetle wheels his droning flight,
And drowsy tinklings lull the distant folds;

Save that from yonder ivy-mantled tow'r
The mopeing owl does to the moon complain
Of such, as wand'ring near her secret bow'r,
Molest her ancient solitary reign.

Beneath those rugged elms, that yew-tree's shade,
Where heaves the turf in many a mould'ring heap,
Each in his narrow cell for ever laid,
The rude Forefathers of the hamlet sleep.

The breezy call of incense-breathing Morn,
The swallow twitt'ring from the straw-built shed,
The cock's shrill clarion, or the echoing horn,
No more shall rouse them from their lowly bed.

For them no more the blazing hearth shall burn,
Or busy housewife ply her evening care:
No children run to lisp their sire's return,
Or climb his knees the envied kiss to share.

Oft did the harvest to their sickle yield,
Their furrow oft the stubborn glebe has broke;
How jocund did they drive their team afield!
How bow'd the woods beneath their sturdy stroke!

Let not Ambition mock their useful toil,
Their homely joys, and destiny obscure;
Nor Grandeur hear with a disdainful smile,
The short and simple annals of the poor.

The boast of heraldry, the pomp of power,
And all that beauty, all that wealth e'er gave,
Await alike the inevitable hour.
The paths of glory lead but to the grave.

Thomas Gray (1716–1771)

Sonnet

O shady vales, O fair enriched meads,
    O sacred woods, sweet fields, and rising mountains,
O painted flowers, green herbs, where Flora treads,
    Refreshed by wanton winds and watery fountains;
O all you winged choristers of wood,
    That, perched aloft, your former pains report,
And straight again recount with pleasant mood
    Your present joys in sweet and seemly sort;
O all you creatures whosoever thrive
    On mother earth, in seas, by air or fire,
      More blessed are you than I here under sun.
Love dies in me whenas he doth revive
    In you; I perish under Beauty's ire,
      Where after storms, winds, frosts, your life is won.

Thomas Lodge (1558–1625)

Hares at Play

The birds are gone to bed the cows are still
And sheep lie panting on each old mole hill
And underneath the willows grey-green bough
Like toil a resting – lies the fallow plough
The timid hares throw daylights fears away
On the lanes road to dust and dance and play
Then dabble in the grain by naught deterred
To lick the dewfall from the barleys beard
Then out they sturt again and round the hill
Like happy thoughts – dance – squat – and loiter still
Till milking maidens in the early morn
Jingle their yokes and sturt them in the corn
Through well known beaten paths each nimbling hare
Sturts quick as fear – and seeks its hidden lair.

John Clare (1793–1864)

Leisure

What is this life, if full of care,
We have no time to stand and stare.

No time to stand beneath the boughs
And stare as long as sheep or cows.

No time to see, when woods we pass,
Where squirrels hide their nuts in grass.

No time to see, in broad daylight,
Streams full of stars like skies at night.

No time to turn at Beauty's glance,
And watch her feet, how they can dance.

No time to wait till her mouth can
Enrich that smile her eyes began.

A poor life this if, full of care,
We have no time to stand and stare.

W. H. Davies (1871–1940)

Tall Nettles

Tall nettles cover up, as they have done
These many springs, the rusty harrow, the plough
Long worn out, and the roller made of stone:
Only the elm butt tops the nettles now.

This corner of the farmyard I like most:
As well as any bloom upon a flower
I like the dust on the nettles, never lost
Except to prove the sweetness of a shower.

Edward Thomas (1878–1917)

Green

Our zummer way to church did wind about
The cliff, where ivy on the ledge wer green.

Our zummer way to town did skirt the wood,
Where sheenèn leaves in tree an' hedge wer green.

Our zummer way to milkèn in the mead,
Wer on by brook, where fluttrèn zedge wer green.

Our hwomeward ways did all run into one,
Where moss upon the roofstwones' edge were green.

William Barnes (1801–1886)

The Dog and the Water-lily

NO FABLE

The noon was shady, and soft airs
    Swept Ouse's silent tide,
When, 'scaped from literary cares,
    I wander'd on his side.

My spaniel, prettiest of his race,
    And high in pedigree
(Two nymphs, adorn'd with ev'ry grace
    That spaniel found for me)

Now wanton'd lost in flags and reeds,
    Now starting into sight
Pursued the swallow o'er the meads
    With scarce a slower flight.

It was the time when Ouse display'd
    His lilies newly blown;
Their beauties I intent survey'd;
And one I wish'd my own.

With cane extended far I sought
    To steer it close to land;
But still the prize, though nearly caught,
    Escap'd my eager hand.

Beau mark'd my unsuccessful pains
    With fixt consid'rate face,
And puzzling set his puppy brains
    To comprehend the case.

But with a chirrup clear and strong
    Dispersing all his dream,
I thence withdrew, and follow'd long
    The windings of the stream.

My ramble finish'd, I return'd.
    Beau, trotting far before
The floating wreath again discern'd,
And plunging left the shore.

I saw him with that lily cropp'd
    Impatient swim to meet
My quick approach, and soon he dropp'd
    The treasure at my feet.

Charm'd with the sight, the world, I cried,
    Shall hear of this thy deed,
My dog shall mortify the pride
    Of man's superior breed;

But chief myself I will enjoin,
    Awake at duty's call,
To show a love as prompt as thine
    To Him who gives me all.

William Cowper (1731–1800)

Into my heart an air that kills

FROM *A SHROPSHIRE LAD*, XL

Into my heart an air that kills
    From yon far country blows:
What are those blue remembered hills,
    What spires, what farms are those?

That is the land of lost content,
    I see it shining plain,
The happy highways where I went
    And cannot come again.

A. E. Housman (1859–1936)

A Drop Fell

A Drop fell on the Apple Tree –
Another – on the Roof –
A Half a Dozen kissed the Eaves –
And made the Gables laugh –

A few went out to help the Brook
That went to help the Sea –
Myself Conjectured were they Pearls –
What Necklaces could be –

The Dust replaced, in Hoisted Roads –
The Birds jocoser sung –
The Sunshine threw his Hat away –
The Bushes – spangles flung –

The Breezes brought dejected Lutes –
And bathed them in the Glee –
Then Orient showed a single Flag,
And signed the Fete away –

Emily Dickinson (1830–1886)

The Grasshopper

Happy insect, what can be
In happiness compared to thee?
Fed with nourishment divine,
The dewy morning's gentle wine!
Nature waits upon thee still,
And thy verdant cup does fill;
'Tis filled where ever thou dost tread,
Nature self's thy Ganymede.
Thou dost drink, and dance, and sing,
Happier than the happiest king!
All the fields which thou dost see,
All the plants belong to thee;
All that summer hours produce,
Fertile made with early juice.
Man for thee does sow and plough;
Farmer he, and landlord thou!
Thou dost innocently joy,
Nor does thy luxury destroy;
The shepherd gladly heareth thee,
More harmonious than he.
Thee country hinds with gladness hear,
Prophet of the ripened year!
Thee Phoebus loves, and does inspire;
Phoebus is himself thy sire.
To thee of all things upon Earth,
Life is no longer then thy mirth.
Happy insect, happy thou,
Dost neither age, nor winter know.

But when thou'st drunk, and danced, and sung,

Thy fill the flowery leaves among

(Voluptuous and wise withal,

Epicuraean animal!)

Sated with thy summer feast,

Thou retir'st to endless rest.

Abraham Cowley (1618–1667)

The Common Cormorant

The common cormorant or shag
Lays eggs inside a paper bag.
The reason you will see no doubt,
Is to keep the lightning out.
But what these unobservant birds
Have never noticed is that herds
Of wandering bears may come with buns
And steal the bags to hold the crumbs.

Christopher Isherwood (1904–1986)

The Wood of August

The wood gathers strength of green in mid-August
Calling from the deep all store of April water
And later, to be triumphant while the time serves;
Golden-rod, orchis, guelder rose and scabious
Grow near him, and he watches the three swerves
Of Cotswold Edge, South Severn and Malvern Sideways.
Soon he will change, the nuts will ripen, and tideways
Turn greater to the equinox, and brown and brittle
His leaves, save the little, will change, and he'll dream
Of two things: how in rich music is fixed his glow
(Ruddy and bronze), and in All Hallows his August title
With vanished days to it, is held as high as any
(Poor un-named English company),
That haws last through November and dare winter's battle.

Ivor Gurney (1890–1937)

The Grasshopper

Grasshopper thrice-happy! who
Sipping the cool morning dew,
Queen-like chirpest all the day
Seated on some verdant spray;
Thine is all what ere earth brings,
Or the howrs with laden wings;
Thee, the Ploughman calls his Joy,
'Cause thou nothing dost destroy:
Thou by all art honour'd; All
Thee the Springs sweet Prophet call;
By the Muses thou admir'd,
By *Apollo* art inspir'd,
Agelesse, ever singing, good,
Without passion, flesh or blood;
Oh how near thy happy state
Comes the Gods to imitate!

Thomas Stanley (1625–1678)

The Owl

I heard the hooting of the White Owl,
Not as far off as the sea,
And in the sultry passion of the night
I knew not what came to me;
Only the voice of an inhuman thing
Thrilled in my ears,
And I stood lonely, listening,
As if from the eternal years
The Owls had hooted, as if the Owls had sinned
And had eaten some insane root,
The moon, the night, the mystery of the wind,
Myself, and the White Owl's hoot.

Arthur Symons (1865–1945)

To Penshurst

LINES 1–44

Thou art not, Penshurst, built to envious show,
    Of touch or marble; nor canst boast a row
Of polished pillars, or a roof of gold;
    Thou hast no lantern, whereof tales are told,
Or stair, or courts; but stand'st an ancient pile,
    And, these grudged at, art reverenced the while.
Thou joy'st in better marks, of soil, of air,
    Of wood, of water; therein thou art fair.
Thou hast thy walks for health, as well as sport;
    Thy mount, to which the dryads do resort,
Where Pan and Bacchus their high feasts have made,
    Beneath the broad beech and the chestnut shade;
That taller tree, which of a nut was set
    At his great birth where all the Muses met.
There in the writhèd bark are cut the names
    Of many a sylvan, taken with his flames;
And thence the ruddy satyrs oft provoke
    The lighter fauns to reach thy Lady's Oak.
Thy copse too, named of Gamage, thou hast there,
    That never fails to serve thee seasoned deer
When thou wouldst feast or exercise thy friends.
    The lower land, that to the river bends,
Thy sheep, thy bullocks, kine, and calves do feed;
    The middle grounds thy mares and horses breed.
Each bank doth yield thee conies; and the tops,
    Fertile of wood, Ashore and Sidney's copse,
To crown thy open table, doth provide
    The purpled pheasant with the speckled side;
The painted partridge lies in every field,
    And for thy mess is willing to be killed.

And if the high-swollen Medway fail thy dish,
  Thou hast thy ponds, that pay thee tribute fish,
Fat aged carps that run into thy net,
  And pikes, now weary their own kind to eat,
As loath the second draught or cast to stay,
  Officiously at first themselves betray;
Bright eels that emulate them, and leap on land
  Before the fisher, or into his hand.
Then hath thy orchard fruit, thy garden flowers,
  Fresh as the air, and new as are the hours.
The early cherry, with the later plum,
  Fig, grape, and quince, each in his time doth come;
The blushing apricot and woolly peach
  Hang on thy walls, that every child may reach.

Ben Jonson (c. 1572–1637)

The Lady of Shalott

PART I

On either side the river lie
Long fields of barley and of rye,
That clothe the wold and meet the sky;
And thro' the field the road runs by
    To many-tower'd Camelot;
And up and down the people go,
Gazing where the lilies blow
Round an island there below,
    The island of Shalott.

Willows whiten, aspens quiver,
Little breezes dusk and shiver
Thro' the wave that runs for ever
By the island in the river
    Flowing down to Camelot.
Four gray walls and four gray towers,
Overlook a space of flowers,
And the silent isle imbowers
    The Lady of Shalott.

By the margin, willow-veil'd,
Slide the heavy barges trail'd
By slow horses; and unhail'd
The shallop flitteth silken-sail'd
    Skimming down to Camelot:
But who hath seen her wave her hand?
Or at the casement seen her stand?
Or is she known in all the land,
    The Lady of Shalott?

Only reapers, reaping early
In among the bearded barley,
Hear a song that echoes cheerly
From the river winding clearly,
    Down to tower'd Camelot:
And by the moon the reaper weary,
Piling sheaves in uplands airy,
Listening, whispers ''Tis the fairy
    Lady of Shalott.'

Alfred, Lord Tennyson (1809–1892)

A Forsaken Garden

In a coign of the cliff between lowland and highland,
    At the sea-down's edge between windward and lee,
Walled round with rocks as an inland island,
    The ghost of a garden fronts the sea.
A girdle of brushwood and thorn encloses
    The steep square slope of the blossomless bed
Where the weeds that grew green from the graves of its roses
    Now lie dead.

The fields fall southward, abrupt and broken,
    To the low last edge of the long lone land.
If a step should sound or a word be spoken,
    Would a ghost not rise at the strange guest's hand?
So long have the grey bare walks lain guestless,
    Through branches and briars if a man make way,
He shall find no life but the sea-wind's, restless
    Night and day.

The dense hard passage is blind and stifled
    That crawls by a track none turn to climb
To the strait waste place that the years have rifled
    Of all but the thorns that are touched not of time.
The thorns he spares when the rose is taken;
    The rocks are left when he wastes the plain.
The wind that wanders, the weeds wind-shaken,
    These remain.

Not a flower to be pressed of the foot that falls not;
    As the heart of a dead man the seed-plots are dry;
From the thicket of thorns whence the nightingale calls not,
    Could she call, there were never a rose to reply.

Over the meadows that blossom and wither
    Rings but the note of a sea-bird's song;
Only the sun and the rain come hither
    All year long.

The sun burns sere and the rain dishevels
    One gaunt bleak blossom of scentless breath.
Only the wind here hovers and revels
    In a round where life seems barren as death.
Here there was laughing of old, there was weeping,
    Haply, of lovers none ever will know,
Whose eyes went seaward a hundred sleeping
    Years ago.

Heart handfast in heart as they stood, 'Look thither,'
    Did he whisper? 'look forth from the flowers to the sea;
For the foam-flowers endure when the rose-blossoms wither,
    And men that love lightly may die – but we?'
And the same wind sang and the same waves whitened,
    And or ever the garden's last petals were shed,
In the lips that had whispered, the eyes that had lightened,
    Love was dead.

Or they loved their life through, and then went whither?
    And were one to the end – but what end who knows?
Love deep as the sea as a rose must wither,
    As the rose-red seaweed that mocks the rose.
Shall the dead take thought for the dead to love them?
    What love was ever as deep as a grave?
They are loveless now as the grass above them
    Or the wave.

All are at one now, roses and lovers,
    Not known of the cliffs and the fields and the sea.
Not a breath of the time that has been hovers
    In the air now soft with a summer to be.
Not a breath shall there sweeten the seasons hereafter
    Of the flowers or the lovers that laugh now or weep,
When as they that are free now of weeping and laughter
    We shall sleep.

Here death may deal not again for ever;
    Here change may come not till all change end.
From the graves they have made they shall rise up never,
    Who have left nought living to ravage and rend.
Earth, stones, and thorns of the wild ground growing,
    While the sun and the rain live, these shall be;
Till a last wind's breath upon all these blowing
    Roll the sea.

Till the slow sea rise and the sheer cliff crumble,
    Till terrace and meadow the deep gulfs drink,
Till the strength of the waves of the high tides humble
    The fields that lessen, the rocks that shrink,
Here now in his triumph where all things falter,
    Stretched out on the spoils that his own hand spread,
As a god self-slain on his own strange altar,
    Death lies dead.

Algernon Charles Swinburne (1837–1909)

The Glow-worm

FROM *SUMMER, THE SEASONS*

    Among the crooked lanes, on every hedge
The glow-worm lights his gem; and through the dark
A moving radiance twinkles. Evening yields
The world to Night; not in her winter-robe
Of massy Stygian woof, but loose array'd
In mantle dun. A faint erroneous ray,
Glanced from the imperfect surfaces of things,
Flings half an image on the straining eye;
While wavering woods, and villages, and streams,
And rocks, and mountain-tops, that long retain'd
The ascending gleam, are all one swimming scene,
Uncertain if beheld. Sudden to Heaven
Thence weary vision turns; where, leading soft
The silent hours of love, with purest ray
Sweet Venus shines; and from her genial rise,
When daylight sickens till it springs afresh,
Unrival'd reigns, the fairest lamp of night.

James Thomson (1700–1748)

One Shelter'd Hare

FROM *THE TASK*, BOOK III, LINES 334–351

Well – one at least is safe. One shelter'd hare
Has never heard the sanguinary yell
Of cruel man, exulting in her woes.
Innocent partner of my peaceful home,
Whom ten long years' experience of my care
Has made at last familiar; she has lost
Much of her vigilant instinctive dread,
Not needful here, beneath a roof like mine.
Yes – thou may'st eat thy bread, and lick the hand
That feeds thee; thou may'st frolic on the floor
At evening, and at night retire secure
To thy straw couch, and slumber unalarm'd.
For I have gain'd thy confidence, have pledg'd
All that is human in me to protect
Thine unsuspecting gratitude and love.
If I survive thee I will dig thy grave;
And when I place thee in it, sighing say,
I knew at least one hare that had a friend.

William Cowper (1731–1800)

The Scholar Gipsy

VERSES 1–3

Go, for they call you, shepherd, from the hill;
    Go, shepherd, and untie the wattled cotes!
        No longer leave thy wistful flock unfed,
Nor let thy bawling fellows rack their throats,
    Nor the cropp'd herbage shoot another head.
        But when the fields are still,
And the tired men and dogs all gone to rest,
    And only the white sheep are sometimes seen
    Cross and recross the strips of moon-blanch'd green.
Come, shepherd, and again begin the quest!

Here, where the reaper was at work of late –
    In this high field's dark corner, where he leaves
        His coat, his basket, and his earthen cruse,
And in the sun all morning binds the sheaves,
    Then here, at noon, comes back his stores to use –
        Here will I sit and wait,
While to my ear from uplands far away
    The bleating of the folded flocks is borne,
    With distant cries of reapers in the corn –
All the live murmur of a summer's day.

Screen'd is this nook o'er the high, half-reap'd field,
    And here till sun-down, shepherd! will I be.
        Through the thick corn the scarlet poppies peep,
And round green roots and yellowing stalks I see
    Pale pink convolvulus in tendrils creep;
        And air-swept lindens yield
Their scent, and rustle down their perfumed showers
    Of bloom on the bent grass where I am laid,
    And bower me from the August sun with shade;
And the eye travels down to Oxford's towers.

Matthew Arnold (1822–1888)

The Ragwort

Ragwort thou humble flower with tattered leaves
I love to see thee come and litter gold
What time the summer binds her russet sheaves
Decking rude spots in beautys marigold
That without thee were dreary to behold
Sun burnt and bare – the meadow bank the baulk
That leads a waggonway through mellow fields
Rich with the tints that harvests plenty yields
Browns of all hues – and every where I walk
Thy waste of shining blossoms richly shields
The sun tanned sward in splendid hues that burn
So bright and glaring that the very light
Of the rich sunshine doth to paleness turn
And seems but very shadows in thy sight

John Clare (1793–1864)

L'Oiseau Bleu

The lake lay blue below the hill.
    O'er it, as I looked, there flew
Across the waters, cold and still,
    A bird whose wings were palest blue.

The sky above was blue at last,
    The sky beneath me blue in blue.
A moment, ere the bird had passed,
    It caught his image as he flew.

Mary Coleridge (1861–1907)

Sonnet

MADE UPON THE GROVES NEAR MERLOU CASTLE

You well compacted Groves, whose light and shade
    Mixt equally, produce nor heat, nor cold,
    Either to burn the young, or freeze the old,
But to one even temper being made,
Upon a Greene embroidering through each Glade
    An Airy Silver, and a Sunny Gold,
    So cloath the poorest that they do behold
Themselves, in riches which can never fade,
    While the wind whistles, and the birds do sing,
While your twigs clip, and while the leaves do friss,
    While the fruit ripens which those trunks do bring,
    Senseless to all but love, do you not spring
Pleasure of such a kind, as truly is
A self-renewing vegetable bliss?

Edward, Lord Herbert of Cherbury (1582–1648)

High Waving Heather

High waving heather 'neath stormy blasts bending
Midnight and moonlight and bright shining stars
Darkness and glory rejoicingly blending
Earth rising to heaven and heaven descending
Man's spirit away from its drear dungeon sending
Bursting the fetters and breaking the bars

All down the mountain sides wild forest lending
One mighty voice to the life giving wind
Rivers their banks in the jubilee rending
Fast through the valleys a reckless course wending
Wider and deeper their waters extending
Leaving a desolate desert behind

Shining and lowering and swelling and dying
Changing for ever from midnight to noon
Roaring like thunder like soft music sighing
Shadows on shadows advancing and flying
Lightning bright flashes the deep gloom defying
Coming as swiftly and fading as soon

Emily Brontë (1818–1848)

The Downs

O bold majestic downs, smooth, fair, and lonely;
O still solitude, only matched in the skies:
    Perilous in steep places,
    Soft in the level races,
Where sweeping in phantom silence the cloudland flies;
With lovely undulation of fall and rise;
    Entrenched with thickets thorned,
By delicate miniature dainty flowers adorned!

I climb your crown, and lo! a sight surprising
Of sea in front uprising, steep and wide:
    And scattered ships ascending
    To heaven, lost in the blending
Of distant blues, where water and sky divide,
Urging their engines against wind and tide,
    And all so small and slow
They seem to be wearily plodding the way they would go.

The accumulated murmur of soft plashing,
Of waves on rocks dashing and searching the sands,
    Takes my ear, in the veering
    Baffled wind, as rearing
Upright at the cliff, to the gullies and rifts he stands;
And his conquering surges scour out over the lands;
    While again at the foot of the downs
He masses his strength to recover the topmost crowns.

Robert Bridges (1844–1930)

Wind on the Corn

Full often as I rove by path or style,
To watch the harvest ripening in the vale,
Slowly and sweetly, like a growing smile –
A smile that ends in laughter – the quick gale
Upon the breadths of gold-green wheat descends;
While still the swallow, with unbaffled grace,
About his viewless quarry dips and bends –
And all the fine excitement of the chase
Lies in the hunter's beauty: in the eclipse
Of that brief shadow, how the barley's beard
Tilts at the passing gloom, and wild-rose dips
Among the white-tops in the ditches reared:
And hedgerow's flowery breast of lacework stirs
Faintly in that full wind that rocks th' outstanding firs.

Charles Tennyson Turner (1808–1879)

On a Peacock

I

Thou foolish Bird, of Feathers proud,
Whose Lustre yet thine Eyes ne're see:
The gazing Wonder of the Crowd,
Beauteous, not to thy self, but Me!
Thy Hellish Voice doth those affright,
Whose Eyes were charmed at thy sight.

II

Vainly thou think'st, those Eyes of thine
Were such as sleepy *Argus* lost:
When he ws touch'd with rod Divine,
Who late of Vigilance did boast.
Little at best they'll thee avail,
Not in thine *Head*, but in thy *Tayl*.

III

Wisemen do *forward* look to try
What will in *following* Moments come:
Backward thy useless Eyes do ly,
Nor do enquire of *future* doom.
'Nothing can remedy what's past;
Wisedom must guard the present cast.'

IV

Our Eyes are best employ'd at home
Not when they are on others plac'd:
From thine but little good can come,
Which never on thy self are cast:
What can of such a Tool be made:
A *Tayl well-furnish'd*, but an empty *Head*.

Thomas Heyrick (1649–1694)

Haymaking

After night's thunder far away had rolled
The fiery day had a kernel sweet of cold,
And in the perfect blue the clouds uncurled,
Like the first gods before they made the world
And misery, swimming the stormless sea
In beauty and in divine gaiety.
The smooth white empty road was lightly strewn
With leaves – the holly's Autumn falls in June –
And fir cones standing up stiff in the heat.
The mill-foot water tumbled white and lit
With tossing crystals, happier than any crowd
Of children pouring out of school aloud.
And in the little thickets where a sleeper
For ever might lie lost, the nettle creeper
And garden-warbler sang unceasingly;
While over them shrill shrieked in his fierce glee
The swift with wings and tail as sharp and narrow
As if the bow had flown off with the arrow.
Only the scent of woodbine and hay new mown
Travelled down the road. In the field sloping down,
Park-like, to where its willows showed the brook,
Haymakers rested. The tosser lay forsook
Out in the sun; and the long waggon stood
Without its team: it seemed it never would
Move from the shadow of that single yew.
The team, as still, until their task was due,
Beside the labourers enjoyed the shade
That three squat oaks mid-field together made
Upon a circle of grass and weed uncut,
And on the hollow, once a chalk pit, but
Now brimmed with nut and elder-flower so clean.

The men leaned on their rakes, about to begin,
But still. And all were silent. All was old,
This morning time, with a great age untold,
Older than Clare and Cobbett, Morland and Crome,
Than, at the field's far edge, the farmer's home,
A white house crouched at the foot of a great tree.
Under the heavens that know not what years be
The men, the beasts, the trees, the implements
Uttered even what they will in times far hence –
All of us gone out of the reach of change –
Immortal in a picture of an old grange.

Edward Thomas (1878–1917)

Fly Away, Fly Away Over the Sea

Fly away, fly away over the sea,
    Sun-loving swallow, for summer is done;
Come again, come again, come back to me,
    Bringing the summer and bringing the sun.

Christina Rossetti (1830–1894)

When summer's end is nighing

FROM *LAST POEMS*, XXXIX

When summer's end is nighing
 And skies at evening cloud,
I muse on change and fortune
 And all the feats I vowed
 When I was young and proud.

The weathercock at sunset
 Would lose the slanted ray,
And I would climb the beacon
 That looked to Wales away
 And saw the last of day.

From hill and cloud and heaven
 The hues of evening died;
Night welled through lane and hollow
 And hushed the countryside,
 But I had youth and pride.

And I with earth and nightfall
 In converse high would stand,
Late, till the west was ashen
 And darkness hard at hand,
 And the eye lost the land.

The year might age, and cloudy
 The lessening day might close,
But air of other summers
 Breathed from beyond the snows,
 And I had hope of those.

They came and were and are not
  And come no more anew;
And all the years and seasons
  That ever can ensue
  Must now be worse and few.

So here's an end of roaming
  On eves when autumn nighs:
The ear too fondly listens
  For summer's parting sighs,
  And then the heart replies.

A. E. Housman (1859–1936)

As Imperceptibly as Grief

As imperceptibly as Grief
The Summer lapsed away –
Too imperceptible at last
To seem like Perfidy –
A Quietness distilled
As Twilight long begun,
Or Nature spending with herself
Sequestered Afternoon –
The Dusk drew earlier in –
The Morning foreign shone –
A courteous, yet harrowing Grace,
As Guest, that would be gone –
And thus, without a Wing
Or service of a Keel,
Our Summer made her light escape
Into the Beautiful.

Emily Dickinson (1830–1886)

SEPTEMBER

Silver Fruit upon Silver Trees

Song at the Beginning of Autumn

Now watch this autumn that arrives
In smells. All looks like summer still;
Colours are quite unchanged, the air
On green and white serenely thrives.
Heavy the trees with growth and full
The fields. Flowers flourish everywhere.

Proust who collected time within
A child's cake would understand
The ambiguity of this –
Summer still raging while a thin
Column of smoke stirs from the land
Proving that autumn gropes for us.

But every season is a kind
Of rich nostalgia. We give names –
Autumn and summer, winter, spring –
As though to unfasten from the mind
Our moods and give them outward forms.
We want the certain, solid thing.

But I am carried back against
My will into a childhood where
Autumn is bonfires, marbles, smoke;
I lean against my window fenced
From evocations in the air.
When I said autumn, autumn broke.

Elizabeth Jennings (1926–2001)

To Autumn

O Autumn, laden with fruit, and stainèd
With the blood of the grape, pass not, but sit
Beneath my shady roof; there thou may'st rest,
And tune thy jolly voice to my fresh pipe,
And all the daughters of the year shall dance!
Sing now the lusty song of fruits and flowers.

'The narrow bud opens her beauties to
The sun, and love runs in her thrilling veins;
Blossoms hang round the brows of Morning, and
Flourish down the bright cheek of modest Eve,
Till clust'ring Summer breaks forth into singing,
And feather'd clouds strew flowers round her head.

'The spirits of the air live on the smells
Of fruit; and Joy, with pinions light, roves round
The gardens, or sits singing in the trees.'
Thus sang the jolly Autumn as he sat;
Then rose, girded himself, and o'er the bleak
Hills fled from our sight; but left his golden load.

William Blake (1757–1827)

Autumn

The thistle down's flying Though the winds are all still
On the green grass now lying Now mounting the hill
The spring from the fountain Now boils like a pot
Through stones past the counting It bubbles red hot

The ground parched and cracked is Like over baked bread
The greensward all wracked is Bents dried up and dead
The fallow fields glitter Like water indeed
And gossamers twitter Flung from weed unto weed

Hill tops like hot iron Glitter bright i' the sun
And the Rivers we're eying Burn to gold as they run
Burning hot is the ground Liquid gold is the air
Whoever looks round Sees Eternity there.

John Clare (1793–1864)

September 1815

While not a leaf seems faded; while the fields,
With ripening harvest prodigally fair,
In brightest sunshine bask; this nipping air,
Sent from some distant clime where Winter wields
His icy scimitar, a foretaste yields
Of bitter change, and bids the flowers beware;
And whispers to the silent birds, 'Prepare
Against the threatening foe your trustiest shields.'
For me, who under kindlier laws belong
To Nature's tuneful quire, this rustling dry
Through leaves yet green, and yon crystalline sky,
Announce a season potent to renew,
'Mid frost and snow, the instinctive joys of song,
And nobler cares than listless summer knew.

William Wordsworth (1770–1850)

The Sheep Fair

The day arrives of the autumn fair,
    And torrents fall,
Though sheep in throngs are gathered there,
    Ten thousand all,
Sodden, with hurdles round them reared:
And, lot by lot, the pens are cleared,
And the auctioneer wrings out his beard,
And wipes his book, bedrenched and smeared,
And takes the rain from his face with the edge of his hand,
    As torrents fall.

The wool of the ewes is like a sponge
    With the daylong rain:
Jammed tight, to turn, or lie, or lunge,
    They strive in vain.
Their horns are soft as finger-nails,
Their shepherds reek against the rails,
The tied dogs soak with tucked-in tails,
The buyers' hat-brims fill like pails,
Which spill small cascades when they shift their stand
    In the daylong rain.

POSTSCRIPT

Time has trailed lengthily since met
    At Pummery Fair
Those panting thousands in their wet
    And woolly wear:
And every flock long since has bled,
And all the dripping buyers have sped,
And the hoarse auctioneer is dead,
Who 'Going – going!' so often said,
As he consigned to doom each meek, mewed band
    At Pummery Fair.

Thomas Hardy (1840–1928)

To Autumn

I

Season of mists and mellow fruitfulness,
    Close bosom-friend of the maturing sun;
Conspiring with him how to load and bless
    With fruit the vines that round the thatch-eves run;
To bend with apples the moss'd cottage-trees,
    And fill all fruit with ripeness to the core;
        To swell the gourd, and plump, the hazel shells
    With a sweet kernel; to set budding more,
And still more, later flowers for the bees,
Until they think warm days will never cease,
    For Summer has o'er-brimmed their clammy cells.

II

Who hath not seen thee oft amid thy store?
    Sometimes whoever seeks abroad may find
Thee sitting careless on a granary floor,
    Thy hair soft-lifted by the winnowing wind;
Or on a half-reap'd furrow sound asleep,
    Drows'd with the fume of poppies, while thy hook
        Spares the next swathe and all its twined flowers:
And sometimes like a gleaner thou dost keep
    Steady thy laden head across a brook;
    Or by a cyder-press, with patient look,
        Thou watchest the last oozing hours by hours.

III

Where are the songs of Spring? Ay, where are they?
    Think not of them, thou hast thy music too, –
While barred clouds bloom the soft-dying day,
    And touch the stubble-plains with rosy hue;
Then in a wilful choir the small gnats mourn
    Among the river sallows, borne aloft
        Or sinking as the light wind lives or dies;
And full-grown lambs loud bleat from hilly bourn;
    Hedge-crickets sing; and now with treble soft
    The red-breast whistles from a garden-croft;
        And gathering swallows twitter in the skies.

John Keats (1795–1821)

Winter will Follow

The heaving roses of the hedge are stirred
By the sweet breath of summer, and the bird
Makes from within his jocund voice be heard.

The winds that kiss the roses sweep the sea
Of uncut grass, whose billows rolling free
Half drown the hedges which part lea from lea.

But soon shall look the wondering roses down
Upon an empty field cut close and brown,
That lifts no more its height against their own.

And in a little while those roses bright,
Leaf after leaf, shall flutter from their height,
And on the reaped field lie pink and white.

And yet again the bird that sings so high
Shall ask the snow for alms with piteous cry,
Take fright in his bewildering bower, and die.

Richard Watson Dixon (1833–1900)

September

FROM *THE EARTHLY PARADISE*

O come at last, to whom the spring-tide's hope
Looked for through blossoms, what hast thou for me?
Green grows the grass upon the dewy slope
Beneath thy gold-hung, grey-leaved apple-tree
Moveless, e'en as the autumn fain would be
That shades its sad eyes from the rising sun
And weeps at eve because the day is done.

What vision wilt thou give me, autumn morn,
To make thy pensive sweetness more complete?
What tale, ne'er to be told, of folk unborn?
What images of grey-clad damsels sweet
Shall cross thy sward with dainty noiseless feet?
What nameless shamefast longings made alive,
Soft-eyed September, will thy sad heart give?

Look long, O longing eyes, and look in vain!
Strain idly, aching heart, and yet be wise,
And hope no more for things to come again
That thou beholdest once with careless eyes!
Like a new-wakened man thou art, who tries
To dream again the dream that made him glad
When in his arms his loving love he had.

William Morris (1834–1896)

Autumn Walk

FROM *TALES OF THE HALL, BOOK IV, THE ADVENTURES OF RICHARD*

It was a fair and mild autumnal sky,
And earth's ripe treasures met th' admiring eye,
As a rich beauty, when her bloom is lost,
Appears with more magnificence and cost:
The wet and heavy grass, where feet had stray'd,
Not yet erect, the wanderer's way betray'd:
Showers of the night had swell'd the deep'ning rill,
The morning breeze had urged the quick'ning mill,
Assembled rooks had wing'd their sea-ward flight,
By the same passage to return at night.
While proudly o'er them hung the steady kite,
Then turn'd him back, and left the noisy throng,
Nor deign'd to know them as he sail'd along.
Long yellow leaves, from oziers, strew'd around,
Choked the small stream, and hush'd the feeble sound,
While the dead foliage dropt from loftier trees.

George Crabbe (1754–1832)

A Narrow Fellow in the Grass

A narrow Fellow in the Grass
Occasionally rides –
You may have met Him – did you not
His notice sudden is –

The Grass divides as with a Comb –
A spotted shaft is seen –
And then it closes at your feet
And opens further on –

He likes a Boggy Acre
A Floor too cool for Corn –
But when a Boy, and Barefoot –
I more than once at Noon

Have passed, I thought, a Whip lash
Unbraiding in the Sun
When stooping to secure it
It wrinkled, and was gone –

Several of Nature's People
I know, and they know me –
I feel for them a transport
Of cordiality –

But never met this Fellow
Attended, or alone
Without a tighter breathing
And Zero at the Bone.

Emily Dickinson (1830–1886)

Autumn

A touch of cold in the Autumn night –
I walked abroad,
And saw the ruddy moon lean over a hedge
Like a red-faced farmer.
I did not stop to speak, but nodded,
And round about were the wistful stars
With white faces like town children.

T. E. Hulme (1883–1917)

Paradise Lost

BOOK IV, LINES 131–165

So on he fares, and to the border comes
Of Eden, where delicious Paradise,
Now nearer, crowns with her enclosure green,
As with a rural mound the champaign head
Of a steep wilderness, whose hairy sides
With thicket overgrown, grotesque and wild,
Access denied; and overhead upgrew
Insuperable height of loftiest shade,
Cedar, and pine, and fir, and branching palm,
A sylvan scene, and as the ranks ascend
Shade above shade, a woody theatre
Of stateliest view. Yet higher then their tops
The verdurous wall of Paradise up-sprung;
Which to our general sire gave prospect large
Into his nether empire neighbouring round.
And higher then that wall a circling row
Of goodliest trees, loaded with fairest fruit,
Blossoms and fruits at once of golden hue,
Appeared, with gay enamelled colours mixed;
On which the sun more glad impressed his beams
Then in fair evening cloud, or humid bow,
When God hath showered the earth: so lovely seemed
That landscape; and of pure now purer air
Meets his approach, and to the heart inspires
Vernal delight and joy, able to drive
All sadness but despair; now gentle gales,
Fanning their odoriferous wings, dispense
Native perfumes, and whisper whence they stole
Those balmy spoils. As when to them who sail
Beyond the Cape of Hope, and now are past

Mozàmbique, off at sea north-east winds blow
Sabean odours from the spicy shore
Of Arabie the Blest, with such delay
Well pleased they slack their course, and many a league
Cheered with the grateful smell old Ocean smiles.

John Milton (1608–1674)

Under the Surface

I
On the surface, foam and roar,
    Restless heave and passionate dash,
Shingle rattle along the shore,
    Gathering boom and thundering crash.

Under the surface, soft green light,
    A hush of peace and an endless calm,
Winds and waves from a choral height,
    Falling sweet as a far-off psalm.

On the surface, swell and swirl,
    Tossing weed and drifting waif,
Broken spars that the mad waves whirl,
    Where wreck-watching rocks they chafe.

Under the surface, loveliest forms,
    Feathery fronds with crimson curl,
Treasures too deep for the raid of storms,
    Delicate coral and hidden pearl.

II
On the surface, lilies white,
    A painted skiff with a singing crew,
Sky-reflections soft and bright,
    Tremulous crimson, gold and blue.

Under the surface, life in death,
    Slimy tangle and oozy moans,
Creeping things with watery breath,
    Blackening roots and whitening bones.

On the surface a shining reach,
    A crystal couch for the moonbeams' rest,
Starry ripples along the beach,
    Sunset songs from the breezy west.

Under the surface, glooms and fears,
    Treacherous currents swift and strong,
Deafening rush in the drowning ears:
    Have ye rightly read my song?

Frances Ridley Havergal (1836–1879)

Ode to the West Wind

PART I

O wild West Wind, thou breath of Autumn's being,
Thou, from whose unseen presence the leaves dead
Are driven, like ghosts from an enchanter fleeing,

Yellow, and black, and pale, and hectic red,
Pestilence-stricken multitudes: O thou,
Who chariotest to their dark wintry bed

The wingèd seeds, where they lie cold and low,
Each like a corpse within its grave, until
Thine azure sister of the Spring shall blow

Her clarion o'er the dreaming earth, and fill
(Driving sweet buds like flocks to feed in air)
With living hues and odours plain and hill:

Wild Spirit, which art moving everywhere;
Destroyer and preserver; hear, oh, hear!

Percy Bysshe Shelley (1792–1822)

Aspens

All day and night, save winter, every weather,
Above the inn, the smithy, and the shop,
The aspens at the cross-roads talk together
Of rain, until their last leaves fall from the top.

Out of the blacksmith's cavern comes the ringing
Of hammer, shoe, and anvil; out of the inn
The clink, the hum, the roar, the random singing –
The sounds that for these fifty years have been.

The whisper of the aspens is not drowned,
And over lightless pane and footless road,
Empty as sky, with every other sound
Not ceasing, calls their ghosts from their abode,

A silent smithy, a silent inn, nor fails
In the bare moonlight or the thick-furred gloom,
In tempest or the night of nightingales,
To turn the cross-roads to a ghostly room.

And it would be the same were no house near.
Over all sorts of weather, men, and times,
Aspens must shake their leaves and men may hear
But need not listen, more than to my rhymes.

Whatever wind blows, while they and I have leaves
We cannot other than an aspen be
That ceaselessly, unreasonably grieves,
Or so men think who like a different tree.

Edward Thomas (1878–1917)

Satyr's Song

FROM *THE FAITHFUL SHEPHERDESS*, EXTRACT ACT IV, SCENE I

    See the day begins to break,
And the light shoots like a streak
Of subtle fire, the wind blows cold,
Whilst the morning doth unfold;
Now the Birds begin to rouse,
And the Squirril from the boughs
Leaps, to get him Nuts and fruit;
The early Lark, that erst was mute,
Carrols to the rising day
Many a note and many a lay.

John Fletcher (1579–1625)

The Loch Ness Monster's Song

Sssnnnwhufffll?
Hnwhuffl hhnnwfl hnfl hfl?
Gdroblboblhobngbl gbl gl g g g g glbgl.
Drublhaflablhaflubhafgabhaflhafl fl fl –
gm grawwwww grf grawf awfgm graw gm.
Hovoplodok – doplodovok – plovodokot-doplodokosh?
Splgraw fok fok splgrafhatchgabrlgabrl fok splfok!
Zgra kra gka fok!
Grof grawff gahf?
Gombl mbl bl –
blm plm,
blm plm,
blm plm,
blp.

Edwin Morgan (1920–2010)

Silver

Slowly, silently, now the moon
Walks the night in her silver shoon;
This way, and that, she peers, and sees
Silver fruit upon silver trees;
One by one the casements catch
Her beams beneath the silvery thatch;
Couched in his kennel, like a log,
With paws of silver sleeps the dog;
From their shadowy cote the white breasts peep
Of doves in a silver-feathered sleep;
A harvest mouse goes scampering by,
With silver claws, and silver eye;
And moveless fish in the water gleam,
By silver reeds in a silver stream.

Walter de la Mare (1873–1956)

Nesting Birds

FROM *SOLOMON ON THE VANITY OF THE WORLD,
KNOWLEDGE, BOOK I: THE ARGUMENT*

Of Birds, how each according to her Kind
Proper Materials for her Nest can find;
And build a Frame, which deepest Thought in Man
Would or amend, or imitate in vain.
How in small Flights They know to try their Young,
And teach the callow Child her Parent's Song.
Why these frequent the Plain, and those the Wood,
Why ev'ry Land has her specific Brood.
Where the tall *Crane*, or winding *Swallow* goes,
Fearful of gathering Winds, and falling Snows:
If into Rocks, or hollow Trees they creep,
In temporary Death confin'd to Sleep;
Or conscious of the coming Evil, fly
To milder Regions, and a Southern Sky.

Matthew Prior (1664–1721)

The Forest

PEAR-TREE

By woodsman's edge I faint and fail;
By craftsman's edge I tell the tale.

CHESTNUT-TREE

High in the wood, high o'er the hall,
Aloft I rise when low I fall.

OAK-TREE

Unmoved I stand what wind may blow.
Swift, swift before the wind I go.

William Morris (1834–1896)

The Harvest Moon

It is the Harvest Moon! On gilded vanes
    And roofs of villages, on woodland crests
    And their aerial neighborhoods of nests
    Deserted, on the curtained window-panes
Of rooms where children sleep, on country lanes
    And harvest-fields, its mystic splendor rests!
    Gone are the birds that were our summer guests,
    With the last sheaves return the laboring wains!
All things are symbols: the external shows
    Of Nature have their image in the mind,
    As flowers and fruits and falling of the leaves;
The song-birds leave us at the summer's close,
    Only the empty nests are left behind,
    And pipings of the quail among the sheaves.

Henry Wadsworth Longfellow (1807–1882)

The Harvest Moon

The flame-red moon, the harvest moon,
Rolls along the hills, gently bouncing,
A vast balloon,
Till it takes off, and sinks upward
To lie in the bottom of the sky, like a gold doubloon.

The harvest moon has come,
Booming softly through heaven, like a bassoon.
And earth replies all night, like a deep drum.

So people can't sleep,
So they go out where elms and oak trees keep
A kneeling vigil, in a religious hush.
The harvest moon has come!

And all the moonlit cows and all the sheep
Stare up at her petrified, while she swells
Filling heaven, as if red hot, and sailing
Closer and closer like the end of the world.

Till the gold fields of stiff wheat
Cry 'We are ripe, reap us!' and the rivers
Sweat from the melting hills.

Ted Hughes (1930–1998)

Hurrahing in the Harvest

Summer ends now; now, barbarous in beauty, the stooks arise
    Around; up above, what wind-walks! what lovely behaviour
    Of silk-sack clouds! has wilder, wilful-wavier
Meal-drift moulded ever and melted across skies?

I walk, I lift up, I lift up heart, eyes,
    Down all that glory in the heavens to glean our Saviour;
    And, éyes, heárt, what looks, what lips yet gave you a
Rapturous love's greeting of realer, of rounder replies?

And the azurous hung hills are his world-wielding shoulder
    Majestic – as a stallion stalwart, very-violet-sweet! –
These things, these things were here and but the beholder
    Wanting; which two when they once meet,
The heart rears wings bold and bolder
    And hurls for him, O half hurls earth for him off under his feet.

Gerard Manley Hopkins (1844–1889)

On the Downs

Up on the downs the red-eyed kestrels hover,
Eyeing the grass.
The field-mouse flits like a shadow into cover
As their shadows pass.

Men are burning the gorse on the down's shoulder;
A drift of smoke
Glitters with fire and hangs, and the skies smoulder,
And the lungs choke.

Once the tribe did thus on the downs, on these downs burning
Men in the frame,
Crying to the gods of the downs till their brains were turning
And the gods came.

And to-day on the downs, in the wind, the hawks, the grasses,
In blood and air,
Something passes me and cries as it passes,
On the chalk downland bare.

John Masefield (1878–1967)

September

Now every day the bracken browner grows,
    Even the purple stars
    Of clematis, that shone about the bars,
Grow browner; and the little autumn rose
    Dons, for her rosy gown,
    Sad weeds of brown.

Now falls the eve, and ere the morning sun,
    Many a flower her sweet life will have lost,
    Slain by the bitter frost,
Who slays the butterflies also, one by one,
    The tiny beasts
    That go about their business and their feasts.

Mary Coleridge (1861–1907)

Spring and Fall

TO A YOUNG CHILD

Márgarét, are you gríeving
Over Goldengrove unleaving?
Leáves líke the things of man, you
With your fresh thoughts care for, can you?
Ah! ás the heart grows older
It will come to such sights colder
By and by, nor spare a sigh
Though worlds of wanwood leafmeal lie;
And yet you wíll weep and know why.
Now no matter, child, the name:
Sórrow's spríngs áre the same.
Nor mouth had, no nor mind, expressed
What heart heard of, ghost guessed:
It ís the blight man was born for,
It is Margaret you mourn for.

Gerard Manley Hopkins (1844–1889)

Colinetta

LINES 1–12

Twas when the Fields had shed their golden Grain.
And burning Suns had sear'd the russet Plain;
No more the Rose or Hyacinth were seen,
Nor yellow Cowslip on the tufted Green:
But the rude Thistle rear'd its hoary Crown,
And the ripe Nettle shew'd an irksom Brown.
In mournful Plight the tarnish'd Groves appear,
And Nature weeps for the declining Year.
The Sun, too quickly, reach'd the western Sky,
And rising Vapours hid his ev'ning Eye:
Autumnal Threads around the Branches flew,
While the dry Stubble drank the falling Dew.

Mary Leapor (1722–1746)

A Nimble Squirrel

FROM *BRITANNIA'S PASTORALS*, BOOK ONE, SONG 5, LINES 56–75

Then, as a nimble squirrel from the wood,
Ranging the hedges for his filberd-food,
Sits peartly on a bough his brown nuts cracking,
And from the shell the sweet white kernel taking,
Till with their crooks and bags a sort of boys,
To share with him, come with so great a noise,
That he is forc'd to leave a nut nigh broke,
And for his life leap to a neighbour oak,
Thence to a beech, thence to a row of ashes;
Whilst through the quagmires, and red water plashes,
The boys run dabbling thorough thick and thin;
One tears his hose, another breaks his shin,
This, torn and tatter'd, hath with much ado
Got by the briars; and that hath lost his shoe;
This drops his band; that headlong falls for haste;
Another cries behind for being last;
With sticks and stones, and many a sounding holloa,
The little fool, with no small sport, they follow,
Whilst he, from tree to tree, from spray to spray,
Gets to the wood, and hides him in his dray.

William Browne (c. 1591–c. 1645)

The Swallows

FROM *AUTUMN, THE SEASONS*

When Autumn scatters his departing gleams,
Warn'd of approaching Winter, gather'd, play
The swallow-people; and toss'd wide around,
O'er the calm sky, in convolution swift,
The feather'd eddy floats: rejoicing once,
Ere to their wintry slumbers they retire;
In clusters clung, beneath the mouldering bank,
And where, unpierced by frost, the cavern sweats:
Or, rather, into warmer climes convey'd,
With other kindred birds of season, there
They twitter cheerful, till the vernal months
Invite them welcome back; for, thronging, now
Innumerous wings are in commotion all.

James Thomson (1700–1748)

The Road Not Taken

Two roads diverged in a yellow wood,
And sorry I could not travel both
And be one traveller, long I stood
And looked down one as far as I could
To where it bent in the undergrowth;

Then took the other, as just as fair,
And having perhaps the better claim,
Because it was grassy and wanted wear;
Though as for that the passing there
Had worn them really about the same,

And both that morning equally lay
In leaves no step had trodden black.
Oh, I kept the first for another day!
Yet knowing how way leads on to way,
I doubted if I should ever come back.

I shall be telling this with a sigh
Somewhere ages and ages hence:
Two roads diverged in a wood, and I –
I took the one less travelled by,
And that has made all the difference.

Robert Frost (1874–1963)

OCTOBER

The Fading Many-Coloured Woods

October

Give me October's meditative haze,
Its gossamer mornings, dewy-wimpled eves,
Dewy and fragrant, fragrant and secure,
The long slow sound of farmward-wending wains,
When homely Love sups quiet 'mid his sheaves,
Sups 'mid his sheaves, his sickle at his side,
And all is peace, peace and plump fruitfulness.

Alfred Austin (1835–1913)

Butterfly

Butterfly, the wind blows sea-ward, strong beyond the garden wall!
Butterfly, why do you settle on my shoe, and sip the dirt on my shoe,
Lifting your veined wings, lifting them? big white butterfly!

Already it is October, and the wind blows strong to the sea
from the hills where snow must have fallen, the wind is polished with
    snow.
Here in the garden, with red geraniums, it is warm, it is warm
but the wind blows strong to sea-ward, white butterfly, content on
    my shoe!

Will you go, will you go from my warm house?
Will you climb on your big soft wings, black-dotted,
as up an invisible rainbow, an arch
till the wind slides you sheer from the arch-crest
and in a strange level fluttering you go out to sea-ward, white speck!

Farewell, farewell, lost soul!
you have melted in the crystalline distance,
it is enough! I saw you vanish into air!

D. H. Lawrence (1885–1930)

Resolution and Independence

VERSES I AND II

I

There was a roaring in the wind all night;
The rain came heavily and fell in floods;
But now the sun is rising calm and bright;
The birds are singing in the distant woods;
Over his own sweet voice the Stock-dove broods;
The Jay makes answer as the Magpie chatters;
And all the air is filled with pleasant noise of waters.

II

All things that love the sun are out of doors;
The sky rejoices in the morning's birth;
The grass is bright with rain-drops; – on the moors
The hare is running races in her mirth;
And with her feet she from the plashy earth
Raises a mist, that, glittering in the sun,
Runs with her all the way, wherever she doth run.

William Wordsworth (1770–1850)

October

The green elm with the one great bough of gold
Lets leaves into the grass slip, one by one, –
The short hill grass, the mushrooms small, milk-white,
Harebell and scabious and tormentil,
That blackberry and gorse, in dew and sun,
Bow down to; and the wind travels too light
To shake the fallen birch leaves from the fern;
The gossamers wander at their own will.
At heavier steps than birds' the squirrels scold.
The rich scene has grown fresh again and new
As Spring and to the touch is not more cool
Than it is warm to the gaze; and now I might
As happy be as earth is beautiful,
Were I some other or with earth could turn
In alternation of violet and rose,
Harebell and snowdrop, at their season due,
And gorse that has no time not to be gay.
But if this be not happiness, – who knows?
Some day I shall think this a happy day,
And this mood by the name of melancholy
Shall no more blackened and obscurèd be.

Edward Thomas (1878–1917)

The Wild Swans at Coole

The trees are in their autumn beauty,
The woodland paths are dry,
Under the October twilight the water
Mirrors a still sky;
Upon the brimming water among the stones
Are nine-and-fifty swans.

The nineteenth autumn has come upon me
Since I first made my count;
I saw, before I had well finished,
All suddenly mount
And scatter wheeling in great broken rings
Upon their clamorous wings.

I have looked upon those brilliant creatures,
And now my heart is sore.
All's changed since I, hearing at twilight,
The first time on this shore,
The bell-beat of their wings above my head,
Trod with a lighter tread.

Unwearied still, lover by lover,
They paddle in the cold
Companionable streams or climb the air;
Their hearts have not grown old;
Passion or conquest, wander where they will,
Attend upon them still.

But now they drift on the still water,
Mysterious, beautiful;
Among what rushes will they build,
By what lake's edge or pool
Delight men's eyes when I awake some day
To find they have flown away?

W. B. Yeats (1865–1939)

To the Fringed Gentian

Thou blossom bright with autumn dew,
And colored with the heaven's own blue,
That openest when the quiet light
Succeeds the keen and frosty night.

Thou comest not when violets lean
O'er wandering brooks and springs unseen,
Or columbines, in purple dressed,
Nod o'er the ground-bird's hidden nest.

Thou waitest late and com'st alone,
When woods are bare and birds are flown,
And frosts and shortening days portend
The aged year is near his end.

Then doth thy sweet and quiet eye
Look through its fringes to the sky,
Blue – blue – as if that sky let fall
A flower from its cerulean wall.

I would that thus, when I shall see
The hour of death draw near to me,
Hope, blossoming within my heart,
May look to heaven as I depart.

William Cullen Bryant (1794–1878)

The Snail

To grass, or leaf, or fruit, or wall,
The snail sticks close, nor fears to fall,
As if he grew there, house and all
     Together.

Within that house secure he hides,
When danger imminent betides
Of storm, or other harm besides
     Of weather.

Give but his horns the slightest touch,
His self-collecting power is such,
He shrinks into his house, with much
     Displeasure.

Where'er he dwells, he dwells alone,
Except himself has chattels none,
Well satisfied to be his own
     Whole treasure.

Thus, hermit-like, his life he leads,
Nor partner of his banquet needs,
And if he meets one, only feeds
     The faster.

Who seeks him must be worse than blind,
(He and his house are so combin'd,)
If, finding it, he fails to find
     Its master.

William Cowper (1731–1800)

Calm is the morn

FROM *IN MEMORIAM A. H. H.*

XI
Calm is the morn without a sound,
   Calm as to suit a calmer grief,
   And only thro' the faded leaf
The chestnut pattering to the ground:

Calm and deep peace on this high wold,
   And on these dews that drench the furze,
   And all the silvery gossamers
That twinkle into green and gold:

Calm and still light on yon great plain
   That sweeps with all its autumn bowers,
   And crowded farms and lessening towers,
To mingle with the bounding main:

Calm and deep peace in this wide air,
   These leaves that redden to the fall;
   And in my heart, if calm at all,
If any calm, a calm despair:

Calm on the seas, and silver sleep,
   And waves that sway themselves in rest,
   And dead calm in that noble breast
Which heaves but with the heaving deep.

Alfred, Lord Tennyson (1809–1892)

Autumn Fires

In the other gardens
  And all up the vale,
From the autumn bonfires
  See the smoke trail!

Pleasant summer over
  And all the summer flowers
The red fire blazes,
  The grey smoke towers.

Sing a song of seasons!
  Something bright in all!
Flowers in the summer,
  Fires in the fall!

Robert Louis Stevenson (1850–1894)

Alcaic

Out in the deep wood, silence and darkness fall,
down through the wet leaves comes the October mist;
no sound, but only a blackbird scolding,
making the mist and the darkness listen.

Peter Levi (1931–2000)

To Flush, My Dog

VERSES 1–13

Loving friend, the gift of one,
Who, her own true faith, hath run,
Through thy lower nature;
Be my benediction said
With my hand upon thy head,
Gentle fellow-creature!

Like a lady's ringlets brown,
Flow thy silken ears adown
Either side demurely,
Of thy silver-suited breast
Shining out from all the rest
Of thy body purely.

Darkly brown thy body is,
Till the sunshine, striking this,
Alchemize its dulness, –
When the sleek curls manifold
Flash all over into gold,
With a burnished fulness.

Underneath my stroking hand,
Startled eyes of hazel bland
Kindling, growing larger, –
Up thou leapest with a spring,
Full of prank and curvetting,
Leaping like a charger.

Leap! thy broad tail waves a light ;
Leap! thy slender feet are bright,

Canopied in fringes.
Leap – those tasselled ears of thine
Flicker strangely, fair and fine,
Down their golden inches

Yet, my pretty sportive friend,
Little is't to such an end
That I praise thy rareness!
Other dogs may be thy peers
Haply in these drooping ears,
And this glossy fairness.

But of thee it shall be said,
This dog watched beside a bed
Day and night unweary, –
Watched within a curtained room,
Where no sunbeam brake the gloom
Round the sick and dreary.

Roses, gathered for a vase,
In that chamber died apace,
Beam and breeze resigning –
This dog only, waited on,
Knowing that when light is gone,
Love remains for shining.

Other dogs in thymy dew
Tracked the hares and followed through
Sunny moor or meadow –
This dog only, crept and crept
Next a languid cheek that slept,
Sharing in the shadow.

Other dogs of loyal cheer
Bounded at the whistle clear,
Up the woodside hieing –
This dog only, watched in reach
Of a faintly uttered speech,
Or a louder sighing.

And if one or two quick tears
Dropped upon his glossy ears,
Or a sigh came double, –
Up he sprang in eager haste,
Fawning, fondling, breathing fast,
In a tender trouble.

And this dog was satisfied,
If a pale thin hand would glide,
Down his dewlaps sloping, –
Which he pushed his nose within,
After, – platforming his chin
On the palm left open.

This dog, if a friendly voice
Call him now to blyther choice
Than such chamber-keeping,
'Come out!' praying from the door, –
Presseth backward as before,
Up against me leaping.

Elizabeth Barrett Browning (1806–1861)

Leaves

Leaves of the summer, lovely summer's pride,
    Sweet is the shade below your silent tree,
Whether in waving copses, where ye hide
    My roamings, or in fields that let me see
    The open sky; and whether ye may be
Around the low-stemm'd oak, robust and wide;
Or taper ash upon the mountain side;
    Or lowland elm; your shade is sweet to me.

Whether ye wave above the early flow'rs
    I' lively green; or whether, rustling sere,
    Ye fly on playful winds, around my feet,

In dying autumn; lovely are your bow'rs,
    Ye early-dying children of the year;
    Holy the silence of your calm retreat.

William Barnes (1801–1886)

The Ivy Green

Oh, a dainty plant is the Ivy green,
That creepeth o'er ruins old!
Of right choice food are his meals, I ween,
In his cell so lone and cold.
The wall must be crumbled, the stone decayed,
To pleasure his dainty whim:
And the mouldering dust that years have made
Is a merry meal for him.
Creeping where no life is seen,
A rare old plant is the Ivy green.

Fast he stealeth on, though he wears no wings,
And a staunch old heart has he.
How closely he twineth, how tight he clings,
To his friend the huge Oak Tree!
And slily he traileth along the ground,
And his leaves he gently waves,
As he joyously hugs and crawleth round
The rich mould of dead men's graves.
Creeping where grim death has been,
A rare old plant is the Ivy green.

Whole ages have fled and their works decayed,
And nations have scattered been;
But the stout old Ivy shall never fade,
From its hale and hearty green.
The brave old plant, in its lonely days,
Shall fatten upon the past:
For the stateliest building man can raise,
Is the Ivy's food at last.
Creeping on, where time has been,
A rare old plant is the Ivy green.

Charles Dickens (1812–1870)

Fall Leaves Fall

Fall leaves fall die flowers away
Lengthen night and shorten day
Every leaf speaks bliss to me
Fluttering from the autumn tree
I shall smile when wreaths of snow
Blossom where the rose should grow
I shall sing when night's decay
Ushers in a drearier day.

Emily Brontë (1818–1848)

Something Told the Wild Geese

Something told the wild geese
– It was time to go;
Though the fields lay golden
– Something whispered, – 'Snow.'
Leaves were green and stirring,
– Berries luster-glossed,
But beneath warm feathers
– Something cautioned, – 'Frost.'
All the sagging orchards
– Steamed with amber spice,
But each wild breast stiffened
– At remembered ice.
Something told the wild geese
– It was time to fly –
Summer sun was on their wings,
– Winter in their cry.

Rachel Field (1894–1942)

The Fading Many-colour'd Woods

FROM *AUTUMN, THE SEASONS*

But see the fading many-colour'd woods,
Shade deepening over shade, the country round
Imbrown; a crowded umbrage, dusk and dun,
Of every hue, from wan declining green
To sooty dark. These now the lonesome Muse,
Low-whispering, lead into their leaf-strown walks,
And give the season in its latest view.

James Thomson (1700–1748)

The Mist in the Meadows

The evening oer the meadow seems to stoop
More distant lessens the diminished spire
Mist in the hollows reaks and curdles up
Like fallen clouds that spread – and things retire
Less seen and less – the shepherd passes near
And little distant most grotesquely shades
As walking without legs – lost to his knees
As through the rawky creeping smoke he wades
Now half way up the arches dissappear
And small the bits of sky that glimmer through
Then trees loose all but tops – I meet the fields
And now indistinctness passes bye
The shepherd all his length is seen again
And further on the village meets the eye

John Clare (1793–1864)

Pied Beauty

Glory be to God for dappled things –
    For skies of couple-colour as a brinded cow;
        For rose-moles all in stipple upon trout that swim;
Fresh-firecoal chestnut-falls; finches' wings;
    Landscape plotted and pierced – fold, fallow, and plough;
        And áll trádes, their gear and tackle and trim.

All things counter, original, spare, strange;
    Whatever is fickle, freckled (who knows how?)
        With swift, slow; sweet, sour; adazzle, dim;
He fathers-forth whose beauty is past change:
              Praise him.

Gerard Manley Hopkins (1844–1889)

North Wind in October

In the golden glade the chestnuts are fallen all;
From the sered boughs of the oak the acorns fall:
The beech scatters her ruddy fire;
The lime hath stripped to the cold,
And standeth naked above her yellow attire:
The larch thinneth her spire
To lay the ways of the wood with cloth of gold.

Out of the golden-green and white
Of the brake the fir-trees stand upright
In the forest of flame, and wave aloft
To the blue of heaven their blue-green tuftings soft.

But swiftly in shuddering gloom the splendours fail,
As the harrying North-wind beareth
A cloud of skirmishing hail
The grievèd woodland to smite:
In a hurricane through the trees he teareth,
Raking the boughs and the leaves rending,
And whistleth to the descending
Blows of his icy flail.
Gold and snow he mixeth in spite,
And whirleth afar; as away on his winnowing flight
He passeth, and all again for a while is bright.

Robert Bridges (1844–1930)

The Jackdaw

TRANSLATED BY WILLIAM COWPER

There is a bird who, by his coat,
And by the hoarseness of his note,
　　Might be suppos'd a crow;
A great frequenter of the church,
Where, bishop-like, he finds a perch,
　　And dormitory too.

Above the steeple shines a plate,
That turns and turns, to indicate
　　From what point blows the weather.
Look up – your brains begin to swim,
'Tis in the clouds – that pleases him,
　　He chooses it the rather.

Fond of the speculative height,
Thither he wings his airy flight,
　　And thence securely sees
The bustle and the raree-show,
That occupy mankind below,
　　Secure and at his ease.

You think, no doubt, he sits and muses
On future broken bones and bruises,
　　If he should chance to fall.
No; not a single thought like that
Employs his philosophic pate,
　　Or troubles it at all.

He sees, that this great roundabout –
The world, with all its motley rout,
    Church, army, physic, law,
Its customs and its bus'nesses,
Is no concern at all of his,
    And says – what says he? – Caw.

Thrice happy bird! I too have seen
Much of the vanities of men;
    And, sick of having seen 'em,
Would cheerfully these limbs resign
For such a pair of wings as thine,
    And such a head between 'em.

Vincent Bourne (1695–1747)

Digging

To-day I think
Only with scents, – scents dead leaves yield,
And bracken, and wild carrot's seed,
And the square mustard field;

Odours that rise
When the spade wounds the root of tree,
Rose, currant, raspberry, or goutweed,
Rhubarb or celery;

The smoke's smell, too,
Flowing from where a bonfire burns
The dead, the waste, the dangerous,
And all to sweetness turns.

It is enough
To smell, to crumble the dark earth,
While the robin sings over again
Sad songs of Autumn mirth.

Edward Thomas (1878–1917)

Sea-weed

Sea-weed sways and sways and swirls
as if swaying were its form of stillness;
and if it flushes against fierce rock
it slips over it as shadows do, without hurting itself.

D. H. Lawrence (1885–1930)

The Wind

The Wind begun to rock the Grass
With threatening Tunes and low –
He flung a Menace at the Earth –
A Menace at the Sky.

The Leaves unhooked themselves from Trees –
And started all abroad
The Dust did scoop itself like Hands
And throw away the Road.

The Wagons quickened on the Streets
The Thunder hurried slow –
The Lightning showed a yellow Beak
And then a livid Claw.

The Birds put up the Bars to Nests –
The Cattle fled to Barns –
There came one drop of Giant Rain,
And then, as if the Hands

That held the Dams had parted hold
The Waters Wrecked the Sky,
But overlooked my Father's House –
Just quartering a Tree –

Emily Dickinson (1830–1886)

October

FROM *THE EARTHLY PARADISE*

O love, turn from the unchanging sea, and gaze
Down these grey slopes upon the year grown old,
A-dying mid the autumn-scented haze,
That hangeth o'er the hollow in the wold,
Where the wind-bitten ancient elms enfold
Grey church, long barn, orchard, and red-roofed stead,
Wrought in dead days for men a long while dead.

Come down, O love; may not our hands still meet,
Since still we live to-day, forgetting June,
Forgetting May, deeming October sweet –
– O hearken, hearken! through the afternoon,
The grey tower sings a strange old tinkling tune!
Sweet, sweet, and sad, the toiling year's last breath,
Too satiate of life to strive with death.

And we too – will it not be soft and kind,
That rest from life, from patience and from pain;
That rest from bliss we know not when we find;
That rest from Love which ne'er the end can gain? –
– Hark, how the tune swells, that erewhile did wane!
Look up love! – ah, cling close and never move!
How can I have enough of life and love?

William Morris (1834–1896)

High Wind

The clouds before him rushed, as they
Were racing home to end the day;
The flying hair of the beeches flew
Out of the East as he went through.

Only the hills unshaken stood.
The lake was tossed into a flood;
She flung her curling wavelets hoar
In wrath on the distracted shore.

Which of the elements hath sinned?
What hath angered thee, O wind?
Thou in all the earth dost see
Nought but it enrageth thee!

Mary Coleridge (1861–1907)

Song

The feathers of the willow
Are half of them grown yellow
   Above the swelling stream;
And ragged are the bushes,
And rusty now the rushes,
   And wild the clouded gleam.

The thistle now is older,
His stalk begins to moulder,
   His head is white as snow;
The branches all are barer,
The linnet's song is rarer,
   The robin pipeth now.

Richard Watson Dixon (1833–1900)

The Roaring Frost

A flock of winds came winging from the North,
Strong birds with fighting pinions driving forth
    With a resounding call: –

Where will they close their wings and cease their cries –
Between what warming seas and conquering skies –
    And fold, and fall?

Alice Meynell (1847–1922)

Four Trees

Four Trees – upon a solitary Acre –
Without Design
Or Order, or Apparent Action –
Maintain –

The Sun – upon a Morning meets them –
The Wind –
No nearer Neighbor – have they –
But God –

The Acre gives them – Place –
They – Him – Attention of Passer by –
Of Shadow, or of Squirrel, haply –
Or Boy –

What Deed is Theirs unto the General Nature –
What Plan
They severally – retard – or further –
Unknown –

Emily Dickinson (1830–1886)

The Last Week in October

The trees are undressing, and fling in many places –
On the gray road, the roof, the window-sill –
Their radiant robes and ribbons and yellow laces;
A leaf each second so is flung at will,
Here, there, another and another, still and still.

A spider's web has caught one while downcoming,
That stays there dangling when the rest pass on;
Like a suspended criminal hangs he, mumming
In golden garb, while one yet green, high yon,
Trembles, as fearing such a fate for himself anon.

Thomas Hardy (1840–1928)

On Seeing Two Swallows Late in October

Lone occupiers of naked sky
When desolate november hovers nigh
And all your fellow tribes in many crowds
Have left the village with the autumn clouds
Carless of old affections for the scene
That made them happy when the fields were green
And left them undisturbed to build their nests
In each old chimney like to welcome guests
Forsaking all like untamed winds they roam
And make with summers an unsettled home
Following her favours to the farthest lands
Oer untraced oceans and untrodden sands
Like happy images they haste away
And leave us lonely till another may

But little lingers old esteem detains
Ye haply thus to brave the chilly air
When skies grow dull with winters heavy rains
And all the orchard trees are nearly bare
Yet the old chimneys still are peeping there
Above the russet thatch where summers tide
Of sunny joys gave you such social fare
As makes you haply wishing to abide
In your old dwellings through the changing year
I wish ye well to find a dwelling here
For in the unsocial weather ye would fling
Gleamings of comfort through the winter wide
Twittering as wont above the old fire side
And cheat the surly winter into spring.

John Clare (1793–1864)

The Woods of Westermain

VERSE 1

Enter these enchanted woods,
    You who dare.
Nothing harms beneath the leaves
More than waves a swimmer cleaves.
Toss your heart up with the lark,
Foot at pace with mouse and worm,
    Fair you fare.
Only at the dread of dark
Quaver, and they quit their form:
Thousand eyeballs under hoods
    Have you by the hair.
Enter these enchanted woods,
    You who dare.

George Meredith (1828–1909)

NOVEMBER

The Trees Bow Down their Heads

Autumn Idleness

This sunlight shames November where he grieves
    In dead red leaves, and will not let him shun
    The day, though bough with bough be over-run.
But with a blessing every glade receives
High salutation; while from hillock-eaves
    The deer gaze calling, dappled white and dun,
    As if, foresters of old, the sun
Had marked them with the shade of forest-leaves.

Here dawn to-day unveiled her magic glass;
    Here noon now gives the thirst and takes the dew;
Till eve bring rest when other good things pass.
    And here the lost hours the lost hours renew
While I still lead my shadow o'er the grass,
    Nor know, for longing, that which I should do.

Dante Gabriel Rossetti (1828–1882)

The Oak

Live thy Life,
   Young and old,
Like yon oak,
Bright in spring,
   Living gold;

Summer-rich
   Then; and then
Autumn-changed,
Soberer-hued
   Gold again.

All his leaves
   Fall'n at length,
Look, he stands,
   Trunk and bough
Naked strength.

Alfred, Lord Tennyson (1809–1892)

November

within the abandoned aviary a sound can be heard.
tread lightly now over nettle and briar:
broken corymbs crepitating underfoot;
rusted iron, unyielding in the rain.

a flutter of wings,
then silence.

Joel Knight (1975–)

No!

No sun – no moon!
No morn – no noon –
No dawn – no dusk – no proper time of day –
No sky – no earthly view –
No distance looking blue –
No road – no street – no 't'other side the way' –
No end to any Row –
No indications where the Crescents go –
No top to any steeple –
No recognitions of familiar people –
No courtesies for showing 'em –
No knowing 'em! –
No travelling at all – no locomotion,
No inkling of the way – no notion –
'No go' – by land or ocean –
No mail – no post –
No news from any foreign coast –
No Park – no Ring – no afternoon gentility –
No company – no nobility –
No warmth, no cheerfulness, no healthful ease,
No comfortable feel in any member –
No shade, no shine, no butterflies, no bees,
No fruits, no flowers, no leaves, no birds, –
November!

Thomas Hood (1799–1845)

The Burning of the Leaves

Now is the time for the burning of the leaves.
They go to the fire; the nostril pricks with smoke
Wandering slowly into a weeping mist.
Brittle and blotched, ragged and rotten sheaves!
A flame seizes the smouldering ruin and bites
On stubborn stalks that crackle as they resist.

The last hollyhock's fallen tower is dust;
All the spices of June are a bitter reek,
All the extravagant riches spent and mean.
All burns! The reddest rose is a ghost;
Sparks whirl up, to expire in the mist: the wild
Fingers of fire are making corruption clean.

Now is the time for stripping the spirit bare,
Time for the burning of days ended and done,
Idle solace of things that have gone before:
Rootless hopes and fruitless desires are there;
Let them go to the fire, with never a look behind.
The world that was ours is a world that is ours no more.

They will come again, the leaf and the flower, to arise
From squalor of rottenness into the old splendour,
And magical scents to a wondering memory bring;
The same glory, to shine upon different eyes.
Earth cares for her own ruins, naught for ours.
Nothing is certain, only the certain spring.

Laurence Binyon (1869–1943)

To Meddowes

Ye have been fresh and green,
    Ye have been fill'd with flowers;
And ye the Walks have been
    Where maids have spent their houres.

You have beheld, how they
    With *Wicker Arks* did come
To kisse, and beare away
    The richer Couslips home.

Y'ave heard them sweetly sing,
    And seen them in a Round:
Each Virgin, like a Spring,
    With Hony-succles crown'd.

But now, we see, none here,
    Whose silv'rie feet did tread,
And with dishevell'd Haire,
    Adorn'd this smoother Mead.

Like Unthrifts, having spent,
    Your stock, and needy grown,
Y'are left here to lament
    Your poore estates, alone.

Robert Herrick (1591–1674)

Autumn: A Dirge

I

The warm sun is falling, the bleak wind is wailing,
The bare boughs are sighing, the pale flowers are dying,
    And the Year
On the earth is her death-bed, in a shroud of leaves dead,
    Is lying.
  Come, Months, come away,
  From November to May,
  In your saddest array;
  Follow the bier
  Of the dead cold Year,
And like dim shadows watch by her sepulchre.

II

The chill rain is falling, the nipped worm is crawling,
The rivers are swelling, the thunder is knelling
    For the Year;
The blithe swallows are flown, and the lizards each gone
    To his dwelling;
  Come, Months, come away;
  Put on white, black and gray;
  Let your light sisters play –
  Ye, follow the bier
  Of the dead cold Year,
And make her grave green with tear on tear.

Percy Bysshe Shelley (1792–1822)

Loud without the Wind was Roaring

Loud without the wind was roaring
    Through the waned Autumnal sky;
Drenching wet, the cold rain pouring,
    Spoke of stormy winters nigh.

    All too like that dreary eve
    Sighed within repining grief –
    Sighed at first – but sighed not long
    Sweet – How softly sweet it came!
    Wild words of an ancient song –
    Undefined, without a name –

'It was spring, for the skylark was singing.'
Those words they awakened a spell –
They unlocked a deep fountain whose springing,
Nor Absence, nor Distance can quell.

In the gloom of a cloudy November
They uttered the music of May –
They kindled the perishing ember
Into fervour that could not decay

Awaken on all my dear moorlands,
The wind in its glory and pride!
O call me from valleys and highlands
To walk by the hill-river's side!

It is swelled with the first snowy weather;
The rocks they are icy and hoar
And darker waves round the long heather
And the fern-leaves are sunny no more.

There are no yellow-stars on the mountain,
The bluebells have long died away
From the brink of the moss-bedded fountain,
From the side of the wintry brae –

But lovelier than corn-fields all waving
In emerald and scarlet and gold
Are the slopes where the north-wind is raving
And the glens where I wandered of old –

'It was morning; the bright sun was beaming.'
How sweetly that brought back to me
The time when nor labour nor dreaming
Broke the sleep of the happy and free

But blithely we rose as the dusk heaven
Was melting to amber and blue –
And swift were the wings to our feet given
While we traversed the meadows of dew.

For the moors, for the moors where the short grass
Like velvet beneath us should lie!
For the moors, for the moors where each high pass
Rose sunny against the clear sky!

For the moors, where the linnet was trilling
Its song on the old granite stone –
Where the lark – the wild skylark was filling
Every breast with delight like its own.

What language can utter the feeling
That rose when, in exile afar,
On the brow of a lonely hill kneeling
I saw the brown heath growing there.

It was scattered and stunted, and told me
That soon even that would be gone
It whispered, 'The grim walls enfold me
I have bloomed in my last summer's sun.'

But not the loved music whose waking
Makes the soul of the Swiss die away,
Has a spell more adored and heart-breaking
Than in its half-blighted bells lay –

The spirit that bent 'neath its power
How it longed, how it burned to be free!
If I could have wept in that hour,
Those tears had been heaven to me –

Well, well the sad minutes are moving
Though loaded with trouble and pain –
And sometime the loved and the loving
Shall meet on the mountains again!

Emily Brontë (1818–1848)

November Skies

Than these November skies
Is no sky lovelier. The clouds are deep;
Into their grey the subtle spies
Of colour creep,
Changing that high austerity to delight,
Till even the leaden interfolds are bright.
And, where the cloud breaks, faint far azure peers
Ere a thin flushing cloud again
Shuts up that loveliness, or shares.
The huge great clouds move slowly, gently, as
Reluctant the quick sun should shine in vain,
Holding in bright caprice their rain.
    And when of colours none,
Not rose, nor amber, nor the scarce late green,
Is truly seen, –
In all the myriad grey,
In silver height and dusky deep, remain
The loveliest,
Faint purple flushes of the unvanquished sun.

John Freeman (1880–1929)

Now the leaves are falling fast

FROM *TWELVE SONGS*

VI

Now the leaves are falling fast,
Nurse's flowers will not last,
Nurses to the graves are gone,
But the prams go rolling on.

Whispering neighbours left and right,
Daunt us from our true delight,
Able hands are left to freeze
Derelict on lonely knees.

Close behind us on our track,
Dead in hundreds cry Alack,
Arms raised stiffly to reprove
In false attitudes of love.

Scrawny through a plundered wood
Trolls run scolding for their food,
Owl and nightingale are dumb,
And the angel will not come.

Clear, unscalable, ahead
Rise the Mountains of Instead,
From whose cold cascading streams
None may drink except in dreams.

W. H. Auden (1907–1973)

Old Song

The day is ending, the night descending,
the heart is frozen, the spirit dead;
but the moon is wending her way, attending
to other things that are left unsaid.

D. H. Lawrence (1885–1930)

The Kitten and Falling Leaves

LINES 1–40

That way look, my Infant, lo!
What a pretty baby-show!
See the Kitten on the wall,
Sporting with the leaves that fall,
Withered leaves – one – two – and three –
From the lofty elder-tree!
Through the calm and frosty air
Of this morning bright and fair,
Eddying round and round they sink
Softly, slowly: one might think,
From the motions that are made,
Every little leaf conveyed
Sylph or Faery hither tending, –
To this lower world descending,
Each invisible and mute,
In his wavering parachute.
– But the Kitten, how she starts,
Crouches, stretches, paws, and darts!
First at one, and then its fellow
Just as light and just as yellow;
There are many now – now one –
Now they stop and there are none.
What intenseness of desire
In her upward eye of fire!
With a tiger-leap half way

Now she meets the coming prey,
Lets it go as fast, and then
Has it in her power again:
Now she works with three or four,
Like an Indian conjurer;
Quick as he in feats of art,
Far beyond in joy of heart.
Were her antics played in the eye
Of a thousand standers-by,
Clapping hands with shout and stare,
What would little Tabby care
For the plaudits of the crowd?
Over happy to be proud,
Over wealthy in the treasure
Of her own exceeding pleasure!

William Wordsworth (1770–1850)

Sonnet 73

That time of year thou mayst in me behold
When yellow leaves, or none, or few, do hang
Upon those boughs which shake against the cold,
Bare ruined choirs where late the sweet birds sang.
In me thou seest the twilight of such day
As after sunset fadeth in the west,
Which by and by black night doth take away,
Death's second self, that seals up all in rest.
In me thou seest the glowing of such fire
That on the ashes of his youth doth lie,
As the deathbed whereon it must expire,
Consumed with that which it was nourished by.
    This thou perceiv'st, which makes thy love more strong,
    To love that well which thou must leave ere long.

William Shakespeare (1564–1616)

The Wind

Who has seen the wind?
    Neither I nor you:
But when the leaves hang trembling,
    The wind is passing thro'.

Who has seen the wind?
    Neither you nor I:
But when the trees bow down their heads,
    The wind is passing by.

Christina Rossetti (1830–1894)

Autumn Ploughing

After the ranks of stubble have lain bare,
And field mice and finches' beaks have found
The last spilled seed corn left upon the ground;
And no more swallows miracle in air;

When the green tuft no longer hides the hare,
And dropping starling flights at evening come;
When birds, except the robin, have gone dumb,
And leaves are rustling downwards everywhere;

Then out, with the great horses, come the ploughs,
And all day long the slow procession goes,
Darkening the stubble fields with broadening strips.

Gray sea-gulls settle after to carouse:
Harvest prepares upon harvest's close,
Before the blackbird pecks the scarlet hips.

John Masefield (1878–1967)

To a Mouse

ON TURNING HER UP IN HER NEST, WITH THE PLOUGH, NOVEMBER, 1785

Wee, sleeket, cowran, tim'rous beastie,
O, what a panic's in thy breastie!
Thou need na start awa sae hasty,
    Wi' bickerin brattle!
I wad be laith to rin an' chase thee,
    Wi' murd'ring pattle!

I'm truly sorry man's dominion
Has broken Nature's social union,
An' justifies that ill opinion,
    Which makes thee startle,
At me, thy poor, earth-born companion,
    An' fellow-mortal!

I doubt na, whyles, but thou may thieve;
What then? poor beastie, thou maun live!
A daimen-icker in a thrave
    'S a sma' request:
I'll get a blessin wi' the lave,
    An' never miss 't!

Thy wee-bit housie, too, in ruin!
It's silly wa's the win's are strewin!
An' naething, now, to big a new ane,
    O' foggage green!
An' bleak December's winds ensuin,
    Baith snell an' keen!

Thou saw the fields laid bare an' wast,
An' weary winter comin fast,
An' cozie here, beneath the blast,
    Thou thought to dwell,
Till crash! the cruel coulter past
    Out thro' thy cell.

That wee-bit heap o' leaves an' stibble
Has cost thee monie a weary nibble!
Now thou's turn'd out, for a' thy trouble,
    But house or hald,
To thole the winter's sleety dribble,
    An' cranreuch cauld!

But mousie, thou art no thy-lane,
In proving foresight may be vain:
The best laid schemes o' mice an' men
    Gang aft agley,
An' lea'e us nought but grief an' pain,
    For promised joy!

Still, thou art blest, compared wi' me!
The present only toucheth thee:
But Och! I backward cast my e'e
    On prospects drear!
An' forward though I canna see,
    I guess an' fear!

Robert Burns (1759–1796)

The Sphinx

VERSES 1–8

In a dim corner of my room for longer than my fancy thinks
A beautiful and silent Sphinx has watched me through the
shifting gloom.

Inviolate and immobile she does not rise she does not stir
For silver moons are naught to her and naught to her the suns that reel.

Red follows grey across the air the waves of moonlight ebb and flow
But with the dawn she does not go and in the night-time she is there.

Dawn follows dawn and nights grow old and all the while this
curious cat
Lies couching on the Chinese mat with eyes of satin rimmed with gold.

Upon the mat she lies and leers and on the tawny throat of her
Flutters the soft and silky fur or ripples to her pointed ears.

Come forth my lovely seneschal! so somnolent, so statuesque!
Come forth you exquisite grotesque! half woman and half animal!

Come forth my lovely languorous Sphinx! And put your head upon
my knee!
And let me stroke your throat and see your body spotted like the Lynx!

And let me touch those curving claws of yellow ivory and grasp
The tail that like a monstrous asp coils round your heavy velvet paws!

Oscar Wilde (1854–1900)

At Day-Close in November

The ten hours' light is abating,
    And a late bird wings across,
Where the pines, like waltzers waiting,
    Give their black heads a toss.

Beech leaves, that yellow the noon-time,
    Float past like specks in the eye;
I set every tree in my June time,
    And now they obscure the sky.

And the children who ramble through here
    Conceive that there never has been
A time when no tall trees grew here,
    That none in time will be seen.

Thomas Hardy (1840–1928)

Hoar Frost

In the cloud-gray mornings
I heard the herons flying;
And when I came into my garden,
My silken outer-garment
Trailed over withered leaves.
A dry leaf crumbles at a touch,
But I have seen many Autumns
With herons blowing like smoke
Across the sky.

Amy Lowell (1874–1925)

November Night

Listen ...
With faint dry sound,
Like steps of passing ghosts,
The leaves, frost-crisp'd, break from the trees
And fall.

Adelaide Crapsey (1878–1914)

Inversnaid

This darksome burn, horseback brown,
His rollrock highroad roaring down,
In coop and in comb the fleece of his foam
Flutes and low to the lake falls home.

A windpuff-bonnet of fáwn-fróth
Turns and twindles over the broth
Of a pool so pitchblack, féll-frówning,
It rounds and rounds Despair to drowning.

Degged with dew, dappled with dew
And the groins of the braes that the brook treads through,
Wiry heathpacks, flitches of fern,
And the beadbonny ash that sits over the burn.

What would the world be, once bereft
Of wet and of wildness? Let them be left,
O let them be left, wildness and wet;
Long live the weeds and the wilderness yet.

Gerard Manley Hopkins (1844–1889)

Autumn Mist

So thick a mist hung over all,
Rain had no room to fall;
It seemed a sea without a shore;
The cobwebs drooped heavy and hoar
As though with wool they had been knit;
Too obvious mark for fly to hit!

And though the sun was somewhere else
The gloom had brightness of its own
That shone on bracken, grass and stone
And mole-mound with its broken shells
That told where squirrel lately sat,
Cracked hazel-nuts and ate the fat.

And sullen haws in hedgerows
Burned in the damp with clearer fire;
and brighter still than those
The scarlet hips hung on the briar
Like coffins of the dead dog-rose;
All were as bright as though for earth
Death were a gayer thing than birth.

Andrew Young (1885–1971)

23 NOVEMBER

Lines

The cold earth slept below,
Above the cold sky shone;
And all around, with a chilling sound,
From caves of ice and fields of snow
The breath of night like death did flow
Beneath the sinking moon.

The wintry hedge was black,
The green grass was not seen;
The birds did rest on the bare thorn's breast,
Whose roots, beside the pathway track,
Had bound their folds o'er many a crack
Which the frost had made between.

Thine eyes glowed in the glare
Of the moon's dying light;
As a fen-fire's beam on a sluggish stream
Gleams dimly, so the moon shone there,
And it yellowed the strings of thy tangled hair,
That shook in the wind of night.

The moon made thy lips pale, beloved –
The wind made thy bosom chill –
The night did shed on thy dear head
Its frozen dew, and thou didst lie
Where the bitter breath of the naked sky
Might visit thee at will.

Percy Bysshe Shelley (1792–1822)

After Rain

The rain of a night and a day and a night
Stops at the light
Of this pale choked day. The peering sun
Sees what has been done.
The road under the trees has a border new
Of purple hue
Inside the border of bright thin grass:
For all that has
Been left by November of leaves is torn
From hazel and thorn
And the greater trees. Throughout the copse
No dead leaf drops
On grey grass, green moss, burnt-orange fern,
At the wind's return:
The leaflets out of the ash-tree shed
Are thinly spread
In the road, like little black fish, inlaid,
As if they played.
What hangs from the myriad branches down there
So hard and bare
Is twelve yellow apples lovely to see
On one crab-tree.
And on each twig of every tree in the dell
Uncountable
Crystals both dark and bright of the the rain
That begins again.

Edward Thomas (1878–1917)

November

The mellow year is hastening to its close;
The little birds have almost sung their last,
Their small notes twitter in the dreary blast –
That shrill-piped harbinger of early snows;
The patient beauty of the scentless rose,
Oft with the Morn's hoar crystal quaintly glass'd,
Hangs, a pale mourner for the summer past,
And makes a little summer where it grows:
In the chill sunbeam of the faint brief day
The dusky waters shudder as they shine,
The russet leaves obstruct the straggling way
Of oozy brooks, which no deep banks define,
And the gaunt woods, in ragged, scant array,
Wrap their old limbs with sombre ivy twine.

Hartley Coleridge (1796–1849)

Seed-Time

I
Flowers of the willow-herb are wool;
Flowers of the briar berries red;
Speeding their seed as the breeze may rule,
Flowers of the thistle loosen the thread.
Flowers of the clematis drip in beard,
Slack from the fir-tree youngly climbed;
Chaplets in air, flies foliage seared;
Heeled upon earth, lie clusters rimed.

II
Where were skies of the mantle stained
Orange and scarlet, a coat of frieze
Travels from North till day has waned,
Tattered, soaked in the ditch's dyes;
Tumbles the rook under grey or slate;
Else enfolding us, damps to the bone;
Narrows the world to my neighbour's gate;
Paints me Life as a wheezy crone.

III
Now seems none but the spider lord;
Star in circle his web waits prey,
Silvering bush-mounds, blue brushing sward;
Slow runs the hour, swift flits the ray.
Now to his thread-shroud is he nigh,
Nigh to the tangle where wings are sealed,
He who frolicked the jewelled fly;
All is adroop on the down and the weald.

IV

Mists more lone for the sheep-bell enwrap
Nights that tardily let slip a morn
Paler than moons, and on noontide's lap
Flame dies cold, like the rose late born.
Rose born late, born withered in bud! –
I, even I, for a zenith of sun
Cry, to fulfil me, nourish my blood:
O for a day of the long light, one!

V

Master the blood, nor read by chills,
Earth admonishes: Hast thou ploughed,
Sown, reaped, harvested grain for the mills,
Thou hast the light over shadow of cloud.
Steadily eyeing, before that wail
Animal-infant, thy mind began,
Momently nearer me: should sight fail,
Plod in the track of the husbandman.

VI

Verily now is our season of seed,
Now in our Autumn; and Earth discerns
Them that have served her in them that can read,
Glassing, where under the surface she burns,
Quick at her wheel, while the fuel, decay,
Brightens the fire of renewal: and we?
Death is the word of a bovine day,
Know you the breast of the springing To-be.

George Meredith (1828–1909)

440

The Autumn Robin

VERSE 1

Sweet little Bird in russet coat
    The livery of the closing year
I love thy lonely plaintive note
    And tiney whispering song to hear
While on the stile or garden seat
    I sit to watch the falling leaves
The song thy little joys repeat
    My loneliness relieves.

John Clare (1793–1864)

The Water-fall

With what deep murmurs through times silent stealth
Doth thy transparent, cool, and watry wealth
    Here flowing fall,
    And chide, and call,
As if his liquid, loose Retinue staid
Lingring, and were of this steep place afraid,
    The common pass
    Where, clear as glass,
    All must descend
Not to an end:
But quickned by this deep and rocky grave,
Rise to a longer course more bright and brave.

    Dear stream! dear bank, where often I
    Have sate and pleas'd my pensive eye,
    Why, since each drop of thy quick store
    Runs thither, whence it flow'd before,
    Should poor souls fear a shade or night,
    Who came (sure) from a sea of light?
    Or since those drops are all sent back
    So sure to thee, that none doth lack,
    Why should frail flesh doubt any more
    That what God takes, hee'l not restore?
    O useful Element and clear!
    My sacred wash and cleanser here,
    My first consigner unto those
    Fountains of life where the Lamb goes?
    What sublime truths and wholesome themes,
    Lodge in thy mystical deep streams!
    Such as dull man can never finde
    Unless that Spirit lead his minde

Which first upon thy face did move,
And hatch'd all with his quickning love.
As this loud brook's incessant fall
In streaming rings restagnates all,
Which reach by course the bank, and then
Are no more seen, just so pass men.
O my invisible estate,
My glorious liberty, still late!
Thou art the Channel my soul seeks,
Not this with Cataracts and Creeks.

Henry Vaughan (1621–1695)

Fair is the World

FROM *THE STORY OF THE GLITTERING PLAIN*

Fair is the world, now autumn's wearing,
And the sluggard sun lies long abed;
Sweet are the days, now winter's nearing,
And all winds feign that the wind is dead.

Dumb is the hedge where the crabs hang yellow,
Bright as the blossoms of the spring;
Dumb is the close where the pears grow mellow,
And none but the dauntless redbreasts sing.

Fair was the spring, but amidst his greening
Grey were the days of the hidden sun;
Fair was the summer, but overweening,
So soon his o'er-sweet days were done.

Come then, love, for peace is upon us,
Far off is failing, and far is fear,
Here where the rest in the end hath won us,
In the garnering tide of the happy year.

Come from the grey old house by the water,
Where, far from the lips of the hungry sea,
Green groweth the grass o'er the field of the slaughter,
And all is a tale for thee and me.

William Morris (1834–1896)

The Night is Freezing Fast

LAST POEMS, XX

The night is freezing fast,
    To-morrow comes December;
        And winterfalls of old
Are with me from the past;
    And chiefly I remember
        How Dick would hate the cold.

Fall, winter, fall; for he,
    Prompt hand and headpiece clever,
        Has woven a winter robe,
And made of earth and sea
    His overcoat for ever,
        And wears the turning globe.

A. E. Housman (1859–1936)

DECEMBER

Winter's Wondrous Frost

Now Winter Nights Enlarge

Now winter nights enlarge
    The number of their houres,
And clouds their stormes discharge
    Upon the ayrie towres.
Let now the chimneys blaze
    And cups o'erflow with wine:
Let well-tun'd words amaze
    With harmonie divine.
Now yellow waxen lights
    Shall waite on hunny Love
While youthfull Revels, Masks, and Courtly sights
    Sleepes leaden spels remove.

This time doth well dispence
    With lovers long discourse;
Much speech hath some defence,
    Though beauty no remorse.
All doe not all things well;
    Some measures comely tread,
Some knotted Ridles tell;
    Some Poems smoothly read.
The Summer hath his joyes,
    And Winter his delights;
Though Love and all his pleasures are but toyes,
    They shorten tedious nights.

Thomas Campion (1567–1620)

Winter

The small wind wispers thro the leafless hedge
Most sharp and chill while the light snowey flakes
Rests on each twig and spike of withered sedge
Resembling scattered feathers – vainly breaks
The pale split sunbeam thro the frowning cloud
On winters frowns below – from day to day
Unmelted still he spreads his hoary shroud
In dithering pride on the pale travellers way
Who croodling hastens from the storm behind
Fast gathering deep and black – again to find
His cottage fire and corners sheltering bounds
Where haply such uncomfortable days
Make musical the woodsaps frizzling sounds
And hoarse loud bellows puffing up the blaze.

John Clare (1793–1864)

Decembers Husbandrie

FROM *FIVE HUNDRED POINTS OF GOOD HUSBANDRIE*, VERSES 1–9

O dirtie December
    Forgotten month past,
For Christmas remember,
    Doe now at the last

When frost will not suffer to dike and to hedge,
    then get thee a heat with thy beetle and wedge:
Once Hallowmas come, and a fire in the hall,
    such slivers doo well for to lie by the wall.

Get grindstone and whetstone, for toole that is dull,
    or often be letted and freat bellie full.
A wheele barrow also be readie to have
    at hand of thy servant, thy compas to save.

Give cattle their fodder in plot drie and warme,
    and count them for miring or other like harme.
Young colts with thy wennels together go serve,
    lest lurched by others they happen to sterve.

The rack is commended for saving of doong,
    so set as the old cannot mischiefe the yoong;
In tempest (the wind being northly or east)
    warm barth under hedge is a sucker to beast.

The housing of cattle while winter doth hold,
    is good for all such as are feeble and old:
It saveth much compas, and many a sleepe,
    and spareth the pasture for walke of thy sheepe.

For charges so little much quiet is won,
    if strongly and handsomely al thing be don:
But use to untackle them once in a day
    to rub and to lick them, to drink and to play.

Get trustie to tend them, not lubberlie squire,
    that all the day long hath his nose at the fire.
Nor trust unto children poore cattel to feede,
    but such as be able to helpe at a neede.

Serve riestraw out first, then wheatstraw and pease,
    then otestraw and barlie, then hay if ye please:
But serve them with hay while the straw stover last,
    then love they no straw, they had rather to fast.

Yokes, forks, and such other, let bailie spie out,
    and gather the same as he walketh about.
And after at leisure let this be his heir,
    to beath them and trim them at home by the fier.

Thomas Tusser (c. 1524–1580)

My Cat Jeoffry

FROM *JUBILATE AGNO*, LINES 1–18

For I will consider my Cat Jeoffry.

For he is the servant of the Living God duly and daily serving him.

For at the first glance of the glory of God in the East he worships in his way.

For this is done by wreathing his body seven times round with elegant quickness.

For then he leaps up to catch the musk, which is the blessing of God upon his prayer.

For he rolls upon prank to work it in.

For having done duty and received blessing he begins to consider himself.

For this he performs in ten degrees.

For first he looks upon his fore-paws to see if they are clean.

For secondly he kicks up behind to clear away there.

For thirdly he works it upon stretch with the fore-paws extended.

For fourthly he sharpens his paws by wood.

For fifthly he washes himself.

For sixthly he rolls upon wash.

For seventhly he fleas himself, that he may not be interrupted upon the beat.

For eighthly he rubs himself against a post.

For ninthly he looks up for his instructions.

For tenthly he goes in quest of food.

Christopher Smart (1722–1771)

Where the Lilies Used to Spring

When the place was green with the shaky grass,
    And the windy trees were high;
When the leaflets told each other tales,
    And stars were in the sky;
When the silent crows hid their ebon beaks
    Beneath their ruffled wing –
Then the fairies watered the glancing spot
    Where the lilies used to spring!

When the sun is high in the summer sky,
    And the lake is deep with clouds;
When gadflies bite the prancing kine,
    And light the lark enshrouds –
Then the butterfly, like a feather dropped
    From the tip of an angel's wing,
Floats wavering on to the glancing spot
    Where the lilies used to spring!

When the wheat is shorn and the burn runs brown,
    And the moon shines clear at night;
When wains are heaped with rustling corn,
    And the swallows take their flight;
When the trees begin to cast their leaves,
    And the birds, new-feathered, sing –
Then comes the bee to the glancing spot
    Where the lilies used to spring!

When the sky is grey and the trees are bare,
    And the grass is long and brown,
And black moss clothes the soft damp thatch,
    And the rain comes weary down,
And countless droplets on the pond
    Their widening orbits ring –
Then bleak and cold is the silent spot
    Where the lilies used to spring!

David Gray (1838–1861)

Birds' Nests

The summer nests uncovered by autumn wind,
Some torn, others dislodged, all dark,
Everyone sees them: low or high in tree,
Or hedge, or single bush, they hang like a mark.

Since there's no need of eyes to see them with
I cannot help a little shame
That I missed most, even at eye's level, till
The leaves blew off and made the seeing no game.

'Tis a light pang. I like to see the nests
Still in their places, now first known,
At home and by far roads. Boys knew them not,
Whatever jays and squirrels may have done.

And most I like the winter nests deep-hid
That leaves and berries fell into:
Once a dormouse dined there on hazel-nuts,
And grass and goose-grass seeds found soil and grew.

Edward Thomas (1878–1917)

The Sea

FROM *TALES OF THE HALL, BOOK IV, THE ADVENTURES OF RICHARD*

Pleasant it was to view the sea-gulls strive
Against the storm, or in the ocean dive,
With eager scream, or when they dropping gave
Their closing wings to sail upon the wave:
Then as the winds and waters raged around,
And breaking billows mix'd their deafening sound,
They on the rolling deep securely hung,
And calmly rode the restless waves among.
Nor pleased it less around me to behold,
Far up the beach, the yesty sea-foam roll'd;
Or from the shore upborne, to see on high,
Its frothy flakes in wild confusion fly:
While the salt spray that clashing billows form,
Gave to the taste a feeling of the storm.

George Crabbe (1754–1832)

Robin Redbreast

Robin on a leafless bough,
  Lord in Heaven, how he sings!
Now cold Winter's cruel Wind
  Makes playmates of poor, dead things.

How he sings for joy this morn!
  How his breast doth pant and glow!
Look you how he stands and sings,
  Half-way up his legs in snow!

If these crumbs of bread were pearls,
  I had no bread at home,
He should have them for that song;
  Robin Redbreast, Come.

W. H. Davies (1871–1940)

Elegy

The wood is bare: a river-mist is steeping
    The trees that winter's chill of life bereaves:
Only their stiffened boughs break silence, weeping
        Over their fallen leaves;

That lie upon the dank earth brown and rotten,
    and matted in the soaking wet:
Forgotten with the spring, that is forgotten
        By them that can forget.

Yet it was here we walked when ferns were springing,
    And through the mossy bank shot bud and blade: –
Here found in summer, when the birds were singing,
        A green and pleasant shade.

'Twas here we loved in sunnier days and greener;
    And now, in this disconsolate decay,
I come to see her where I most have seen her,
        And touch the happier day.

For on this path, at every turn and corner,
    The fancy of her figure on me falls:
Yet walks she with the slow step of a mourner,
        Nor hears my voice that calls.

So through my heart there winds a track of feeling,
    A path of memory, that is all her own:
Whereto her phantom beauty ever stealing
        Haunts the sad spot alone.

About her steps the trunks are bare, the branches
  Drip heavy tears upon her downcast head;
And bleed from unseen wounds that no sun stanches,
    For the year's sun is dead.

And dead leaves wrap the fruits that summer planted:
  And birds that love the South have taken wing.
The wanderer, loitering o'er the scene enchanted,
    Weeps, and despairs of spring.

Robert Bridges (1844–1930)

Song

Through springtime walks, with flowers perfumed,
    I chased a wild capricious fair,
Where hyacinths and jonquils bloomed,
    Chanting gay sonnets through the air:
Hid amid a briary dell,
    Or 'neath a hawthorn tree,
Her sweet enchantments led me on,
    And still deluded me.

While summer's splendant glory smiles,
    My ardent love in vain essayed;
I strove to win her heart by wiles,
    But still a thousand pranks she played;
Still o'er each sun-burnt furzy hill,
    Wild, playful, gay and free,
She laughed and scorned, I chased her still,
    And still she bantered me.

When autumn waves her golden ears,
    And wafts o'er fruits her pregnant breath,
The sprightly lark its pinions rears,
    I chased her o'er the daisied heath;
Sweet harebells trembled in the vale,
    And all around was glee;
Still, wanton as the timid hart,
    She swiftly flew from me.

Now winter lights its cheerful fire,
  While jests with frolic mirth resound,
And draws the wandering beauty nigher,
  'Tis now too cold to rove around:
The Christmas game, the playful dance,
  Incline her heart to glee;
Mutual we glow, and kindling love,
  Draws every wish to me.

Anne Batten Cristall (1769–1848)

The Night is Darkening Round Me

VERSES 1–3

The night is darkening round me
The wild winds coldly blow
But a tyrant spell has bound me
And I cannot cannot go

The giant trees are bending
Their bare boughs weighed with snow
The storm is fast descending
And yet I cannot go

Clouds beyond clouds above me
Wastes beyond wastes below
But nothing drear can move me
I will not cannot go

Emily Brontë (1818–1848)

A *nocturnall upon* S. Lucies *day,* *Being the shortest day.*

'Tis the yeares midnight, and it is the dayes,
Lucies, who scarce seaven houres herself unmaskes,
    The Sunne is spent, and now his flasks
    Send forth light squibs, no constant rayes;
        The worlds whole sap is sunke:
The generall balme th' hydroptique earth hath drunk,
Whither, as to the beds-feet life is shrunke,
Dead and enterr'd, yet all these seeme to laugh,
Compar'd with mee, who am their Epitaph.

Study me then, you who shall lovers bee
At the next world, that is, at the next Spring;
    For I am every dead thing,
    In whom love wrought new Alchemie.
        For his art did expresse
A quintessence even from nothingnesse,
From dull privations, and leane emptinesse
He ruin'd mee, and I am re-begot
Of absence, darknesse, death; things which are not.

All others, from all things, draw all that's good,
Life, soule, forme, spirit, whence they beeing have,
    I, by loves limbecke, am the grave
    Of all, that's nothing. Oft a flood
        Have wee two wept, and so
Drownd the whole world, us two; oft did we grow
To be two Chaoses, when we did show
Care to aught else; and often absences
Withdrew our soules, and made us carcasses.

463

But I am by her death (which word wrongs her)
Of the first nothing, the Elixir grown;
    Were I a man, that I were one
    I needs must know, I should preferre,
        If I were any beast,
Some ends, some means; Yea plants, yea stones detest,
And love, all, all some properties invest,
If I an ordinary nothing were,
As shadow, a light and body must be here.

But I am None; nor will my Sunne renew.
You lovers, for whose sake, the lesser Sunne
    At this time to the Goat is runne
    To fetch new lust, and give it you,
        Enjoy your summer all;
Since she enjoyes her long nights festivall,
Let mee prepare towards her, and let mee call
This houre her Vigill, and her eve, since this
Both the yeares, and the dayes deep midnight is.

John Donne (1572–1631)

Speak of the North

Speak of the North! A lonely moor
Silent and dark and trackless swells,
The waves of some wild streamlet pour
Hurriedly through its ferny dells.

Profoundly still the twilight air,
Lifeless the landscape; so we deem,
Till like a phantom gliding near
A stag bends down to drink the stream.

And far away a mountain zone,
A cold, white waste of snow-drifts lies,
And one star, large and soft and lone,
Silently lights the unclouded skies.

Charlotte Brontë (1816–1855)

There was an Old Lady whose Folly

There was an Old Lady whose folly,
Induced her to sit in a holly;
Whereupon by a thorn, her dress being torn,
She quickly became melancholy.

Edward Lear (1812–1888)

Wide o'er the Brim

FROM *WINTER, THE SEASONS*

Wide o'er the brim, with many a torrent swell'd,
And the mix'd ruin of its banks o'erspread,
At last the rous'd-up river pours along:
Resistless, roaring, dreadful, down it comes,
From the rude mountain, and the mossy wild,
Tumbling thro' rocks abrupt, and sounding far;
Then o'er the sanded valley floating spreads,
Calm, sluggish, silent; till again constrain'd
Between two meeting hills it bursts away,
Where rocks and woods o'erhang the turbid stream;
There gathering triple force, rapid, and deep,
It boils, and wheels, and foams, and thunders through.

James Thomson (1700–1748)

Winter

FROM *LOVE'S LABOUR'S LOST*, ACT V, SCENE II

WINTER
When icicles hang by the wall,
    And Dick the shepherd blows his nail;
And Tom bears logs into the hall,
    And milk comes frozen home in pail;
When blood is nipped, and ways be foul,
Then nightly sings the staring owl:
Tu-whit, tu-whoo! – a merry note,
While greasy Joan doth keel the pot.

When all aloud the wind doth blow,
    And coughing drowns the parson's saw:
And birds sit brooding in the snow,
    And Marian's nose looks red and raw;
When roasted crabs hiss in the bowl
Then nightly sings the staring owl:
Tu-whit, tu-whoo! – a merry note,
While greasy Joan doth keel the pot.

William Shakespeare (1564–1616)

It sifts from Leaden Sieves

It sifts from Leaden Sieves –
It powders all the Wood.
It fills with Alabaster Wool
The Wrinkles of the Road –

It makes an Even Face
Of Mountain, and of Plain –
Unbroken Forehead from the East
Unto the East again –

It reaches to the Fence –
It wraps it Rail by Rail
Till it is lost in Fleeces –
It deals Celestial Vail

To Stump, and Stack – and Stem –
A Summer's empty Room –
Acres of Joints, where Harvests were,
Recordless, but for them –

It Ruffles Wrists of Posts
As Ankles of a Queen –
Then stills it's Artisans – like Ghosts –
Denying they have been –

Emily Dickinson (1830–1886)

Dirge in Woods

A wind sways the pines,
    And below
Not a breath of wild air;
Still as the mosses that glow
On the flooring and over the lines
Of the roots here and there.
The pine-tree drops its dead;
They are quiet, as under the sea.
Overhead, overhead
Rushes life in a race,
As the clouds the clouds chase;
    And we go,
And we drop like the fruits of the tree,
    Even we,
    Even so.

George Meredith (1828–1909)

Stanza

If I walk in Autumn's even
   While the dead leaves pass,
If I look on Spring's soft heaven, –
   Something is not there which was
Winter's wondrous frost and snow,
Summer's clouds, where are they now?

Percy Bysshe Shelley (1792–1822)

The Eagle

FRAGMENT

He clasps the crag with crooked hands;
Close to the sun in lonely lands,
Ring'd with the azure world, he stands.

The wrinkled sea beneath him crawls;
He watches from his mountain walls,
And like a thunderbolt he falls.

Alfred, Lord Tennyson (1809–1892)

Stopping by Woods on a Snowy Evening

Whose woods these are I think I know.
His house is in the village though;
He will not see me stopping here
To watch his woods fill up with snow.

My little horse must think it queer
To stop without a farmhouse near
Between the woods and frozen lake
The darkest evening of the year.

He gives his harness bells a shake
To ask if there is some mistake.
The only other sound's the sweep
Of easy wind and downy flake.

The woods are lovely, dark and deep,
But I have promises to keep,
And miles to go before I sleep.
And miles to go before I sleep.

Robert Frost (1874–1963)

The Christmas Life

'IF YOU DON'T HAVE A REAL TREE, YOU DON'T BRING
THE CHRISTMAS LIFE INTO THE HOUSE.'

Josephine Mackinnon, aged 8

Bring in a tree, a young Norwegian spruce,
Bring hyacinths that rooted in the cold.
Bring winter jasmine as its buds unfold –
Bring the Christmas life into this house.

Bring red and green and gold, bring things that shine,
Bring candlesticks and music, food and wine.
Bring in your memories of Christmas past.
Bring in your tears for all that you have lost.

Bring in the shepherd boy, the ox and ass,
Bring in the stillness of an icy night,
Bring in the birth, of hope and love and light.
Bring the Christmas life into this house.

Wendy Cope (1945–)

Green Groweth the Holly

Green groweth the holly,
So doth the ivy.
Though winter blasts blow never so high,
Green groweth the holly.

As the holly groweth green
And never changeth hue,
So I am, ever hath been,
Unto my lady true.

As the holly groweth green
With ivy all alone
When flowers cannot be seen
And greenwood leaves be gone,

Now unto my lady
Promise to her I make,
From all other only
To her I me betake.

Adieu, mine own lady,
Adieu, my special
Who hath my heart truly
Be sure, and ever shall.

King Henry VIII (1491–1547)

The Oxen

Christmas Eve, and twelve of the clock.
 'Now they are all on their knees,'
An elder said as we sat in a flock
 By the embers in hearthside ease.

We pictured the meek mild creatures where
 They dwelt in their strawy pen,
Nor did it occur to one of us there
 To doubt they were kneeling then.

So fair a fancy few would weave
 In these years! Yet, I feel,
If someone said on Christmas Eve,
 'Come; see the oxen kneel

'In the lonely barton by yonder coomb
 Our childhood used to know,'
I should go with him in the gloom,
 Hoping it might be so.

Thomas Hardy (1840–1928)

Christmas Landscape

Tonight the wind gnaws
with teeth of glass,
the jackdaw shivers
in caged branches of iron,
the stars have talons.

There is hunger in the mouth
of vole and badger,
silver agonies of breath
in the nostril of the fox,
ice on the rabbit's paw.

Tonight has no moon,
no food for the pilgrim;
the fruit tree is bare,
the rose bush a thorn
and the ground is bitter with stones.

But the mole sleeps, and the hedgehog
lies curled in a womb of leaves,
the bean and the wheat-seed
hug their germs in the earth
and the stream moves under the ice.

Tonight there is no moon,
but a new star opens
like a silver trumpet over the dead.
Tonight in a nest of ruins
the blessed babe is laid.

And the fir tree warms to a bloom of candles,
and the child lights his lantern,
stares at his tinselled toy;
and our hearts and hearths
smoulder with live ashes.

In the blood of our grief
the cold earth is suckled,
in our agony the womb
convulses its seed;
in the first cry of anguish
the child's first breath is born.

Laurie Lee (1914–1997)

The Sheepdog

After the very bright light,
And the talking bird,
And the singing,
And the sky filled up wi' wings,
And then the silence,

Our lads sez
We'd better go, then.
Stay, Shep. Good dog, stay.
So I stayed wi' t' sheep.

After they cum back,
It sounded grand, what they'd seen:
Camels, and kings, and such,
Wi' presents – human sort,
Not the kind you eat –
And a baby. Presents wes for him.
Our lads took him a lamb.

I had to stay behind wi' t' sheep.
Pity they didn't tek me along too.
I'm good wi' lambs,
And the baby might have liked a dog
After all that myrrh and such.

U. A. Fanthorpe (1929–2009)

The Darkling Thrush

I leant upon a coppice gate
        When Frost was spectre-gray,
And Winter's dregs made desolate
        The weakening eye of day.
The tangled bine-stems scored the sky
        Like strings of broken lyres,
And all mankind that haunted nigh
        Had sought their household fires.

The land's sharp features seemed to be
        The Century's corpse outleant,
His crypt the cloudy canopy,
        The wind his death-lament.
The ancient pulse of germ and birth
        Was shrunken hard and dry,
And every spirit upon earth
        Seemed fervourless as I.

At once a voice arose among
        The bleak twigs overhead
In a full-hearted evensong
        Of joy illimited;
An aged thrush, frail, gaunt, and small,
        In blast-beruffled plume,
Had chosen thus to fling his soul
        Upon the growing gloom.

So little cause for carolings
    Of such ecstatic sound
Was written on terrestrial things
    Afar or nigh around,
That I could think there trembled through
    His happy good-night air
Some blessed Hope, whereof he knew
    And I was unaware.

Thomas Hardy (1840–1928)

Sonnet 97

How like a winter hath my absence been
From thee, the pleasure of the fleeting year!
What freezings have I felt, what dark days seen!
What old December's bareness everywhere!
And yet this time removed was summer's time,
The teeming autumn, big with rich increase,
Bearing the wanton burthen of the prime,
Like widowed wombs after their lords' decease.
Yet this abundant issue seemed to me
But hope of orphans and unfathered fruit;
For summer and his pleasures wait on thee,
And, thou away, the very birds are mute;
    Or, if they sing, 'tis with so dull a cheer,
    That leaves look pale, dreading the winter's near.

William Shakespeare (1564–1616)

In the Bleak Mid-winter

In the bleak mid-winter
    Frosty wind made moan,
Earth stood hard as iron,
    Water like a stone;
Snow had fallen, snow on snow,
    Snow on snow,
In the bleak mid-winter
    Long ago.

Christina Rossetti (1830–1894)

A Winter Song

VERSES 1–6, UNFINISHED

It is early morning within this room; without,
Dark and damp; without and within, stillness
Waiting for day: not a sound but a listening air.

Yellow jasmine, delicate on stiff branches
Stands in a Tuscan pot to delight the eye
In spare December's patient nakedness.

Suddenly, softly, as if at a breath breathed
On the pale wall, a magical apparition,
The shadow of the jasmine, branch and bloom!

It was not there, it is there, in a perfect image;
And all is changed. It is like a memory lost
Returning without a reason into the mind;

And it seems to me that the beauty of the shadow
Is more beautiful than the flower; a strange beauty,
Pencilled and silently deepening to distinctness.

As a memory stealing out of the mind's slumber,
A memory floating up from a dark water,
Can be more beautiful than the thing remembered.

Laurence Binyon (1869–1943)

The Seasons

FROM *THE ART OF PRESERVING HEALTH, BOOK III, EXERCISE*

Observe the circling year. How unperceiv'd
Her seasons change! Behold! by slow degrees,
Stern Winter tamed into a ruder spring;
The ripen'd Spring a milder summer glows;
Departing Summer sheds Pomona's store;
And aged Autumn brews the Winter storm.

John Armstrong (1709–1779)

Index of first lines

486

Index of poets

Acknowledgements

W. H. Auden, 'Twelve Songs VI' from *Collected Shorter Poems 1927–1957* (Faber, 1966). Reproduced with kind permission of Curtis Brown USA.

John Betjeman, 'Winter Seascape' from *Collected Poems* © 1955, 1958, 1962, 1964, 1968, 1970, 1979, 1981, 1982, 2001. Reproduced by permission of John Murray, an imprint of Hodder and Stoughton Ltd.

Amy Clampitt, 'Botanical Nomenclature', from *The Kingfisher* (Knopf, 1983). Reproduced with kind permission of Berkshire Taconic Community Foundation.

Wendy Cope, 'The Christmas Life', taken from *Two Cures for Love*. Copyright © Wendy Cope, 2008.

Walter de la Mare, 'Silver', from *Selected Poems* (Faber, 2006). © The Literary Trustees of Walter de la Mare and the Society of Authors as their Representative.

T. S. Eliot, 'Cape Ann', from *Collected Poems 1909–1962*. Copyright © T. S. Eliot, 1925, 1936, 1963.

U. A. Fanthorpe, 'The Sheepdog', from *U. A. Fanthorpe: New and Collected Poems*, Enitharmon Press, 2010. © Dr R. V. Bailey.

John Foster, 'Spring Snow', from *The Poetry Chest* (Oxford University Press, 2007). © John Foster 2007. Reprinted with permission from Oxford University Press.

Robert Frost, 'Leaves Compared with Flowers', 'Stopping by Woods on a Snowy Day' and 'The Road Not Taken', from *The Complete Poems of Robert Frost* (Cape, 1967). © The Estate of Robert Frost 1967. Reprinted with kind permission of Penguin Random House.

Huge thanks to everyone at Hatchards for looking after my books so well. Thanks to Ian Prince for finding poems, Joel Knight for writing them and the staff at The Saison Poetry Library, in particular Lauren Purchase, for all their help. Nicola Newman and Tina Persaud at Batsford were, as always, wonderful to work with and my agent Teresa Chris has been as supportive as ever. Lastly, thanks to Matilda, for being a perfect paperweight.